BASEBALL
in
PINELLAS COUNTY

Dan Hirshberg

FOREWORD BY TOM KOTCHMAN

THE History PRESS

Published by The History Press
An imprint of Arcadia Publishing
Charleston, SC
www.historypress.com

Copyright © 2025 by Dan Hirshberg
All rights reserved

First published 2025

Manufactured in the United States

ISBN 9781467159487

Library of Congress Control Number: 2025934713

Notice: The information in this book is true and complete to the best of our knowledge. It is offered without guarantee on the part of the author or The History Press. The author and The History Press disclaim all liability in connection with the use of this book.

All rights reserved. No part of this book may be reproduced or transmitted in any form whatsoever without prior written permission from the publisher except in the case of brief quotations embodied in critical articles and reviews.

This book is dedicated to all the great baseball people of Pinellas County, past and present; to all those who endured Hurricanes Helene and Milton in 2024; and to Steve Giorgiadis, whose life and baseball potential was so tragically cut short.

CONTENTS

FOREWORD

I was born in North Dakota and lived in Illinois in my early years. In 1967, when I was thirteen, my family moved to Seminole. I've been here ever since. With the move, baseball changed a lot for me. I was used to only two or three months of baseball, and I realized right away that down here, they take their baseball stuff seriously. I remember going to a Seminole High School playoff game, and the team lost. There were tears afterward. It all made a big impression on me. As a young kid, I played on the local baseball fields; I played high school ball at Seminole; and as a parent, I watched my son, Casey, play ball and my daughter, Christal, softball.

After high school, I played ball for two years at Chipola Junior College and twice got drafted but didn't sign. Then I played at Georgia Southern University for two years, after which I was signed by the Reds as a non-drafted player. I had a brief minor league career that didn't work out. But playing in the minors got my foot in the door to start managing at twenty-four years old. I would manage and coach in the minor leagues and scout for a few major league baseball clubs. I worked first with the Tigers and then the Angels and the Red Sox. My main scouting circuit was the state of Florida. Obviously, though, I had a personal interest in Pinellas County, since it was in my backyard. I spent forty-seven years seeing and evaluating the enormous talent in Florida—and, in many cases, close to home.

Between the weather, the great youth and high school coaching, the competition and, maybe, a little bit of the major league players spring training here rubbing off on some of the young men with aspirations of going to the Show, Pinellas County has a history of "growing" quality ballplayers.

There have been so many outstanding players from Pinellas County—and not all of them became major league stars. Plenty went on to have success in college, whether it was junior college or Division I or II. Many got to the minor leagues, where it can be tough going—and humbling, especially for those who were stars in high school. A good number made it to the majors, as they say, for a cup of coffee. A few did very well in the majors.

It's very hard for even the best to get on a major league field. So many guys seem to have potential. But there's no guarantee, even if you are a high draft pick.

I've seen a lot of changes in Pinellas County and throughout the region. I always liked the way the Pony League worked, with the pitching mound distance and base paths transitioning longer as players got older. I always liked how Little League works. I was so happy to see Lake Mary win the 2024 Little League championship in Williamsport. It seems like Little League doesn't exist as much anymore. I hope that changes. I think some of the leagues for younger kids are too commercialized now. Maybe there's too much emphasis on travel teams—baseball and softball. That's a lot for a young kid and for a family: all that traveling with food, gas, fees and the other expenses that come up. That's especially true of the travel teams that start when the kids are, sometimes, as young as eight years old. It should be more about having fun and less pressure.

When it comes to high school now, there are a lot more options for guys to choose from. Thirty years ago, you pretty much just had the public schools and Clearwater Central Catholic, which is basically a private school. Now you have a lot more schools in the county, some with Astroturf and state-of-the-art training facilities.

I've seen a host of great players emerge from Pinellas. That hasn't changed. When I think about some of the best players—and I'll probably forget a few—I think about Brian Harvey from Dunedin, a first baseman; Bobby Wilson, a catcher from Seminole; Boof Bonser, a legend. He had as much raw power as anybody. He was a man-child, a man among boys. He could throw eighty-eight miles per hour as a pitcher when he was fourteen, and by the time he was a senior in high school, he was touching ninety-six. I once saw him hit an opposite field home run over the right field fence at Seminole. Donnie Scott was another. Larry Jones pitched for Seminole and would go on to Florida State University and then play for a while in the minors.

Arguably, the top two from here are Bill Freehan and Howard Johnson. Freehan, who played for the Detroit Tigers for many years, went to Bishop

Barry High School (now St. Petersburg Catholic High School).* Johnson had a very successful career as a Tiger and a New York Met.

Probably the best pitcher I faced in high school and college was right-hander Danny O'Brien. Oh my goodness, what an imposing pitcher. He made it look so easy. He went to Bishop Barry, too, and then to Florida State University. Danny, whose sister married Bill Freehan, would pitch briefly with the St. Louis Cardinals in 1978 and 1979. I could go on and on: Patrick Boyd, Ryan Webb, Ryan Weber, Toby Hall and Greg Jones, a catcher with one of the best arms I'd ever seen who became a pitcher in the majors. A number of these fantastic players are highlighted in this book.

Also featured in these pages is someone very close to me: my son, Casey! I am proud to say that he had a tremendous career in the major leagues and was known particularly for his excellent defense at first base. He still owns the records for highest career fielding percentage, most consecutive games without an error and most consecutive chances without an error.

I would also like to remind folks of what I consider to be one of the most amazing streaks of high draft picks from the area, which occurred from 1999 to 2004. You had Doug Waechter, who played at Northeast and later with the Rays and is currently one of the game announcers for the Rays. in 1999; Boof Bonser in 2000; Casey and Bobby Wilson, the Player of the Year, in 2001; Brian Dopirak, a first baseman from Dunedin, in 2002; Ryan Harvey, an outfielder from Dunedin, drafted in 2003; and in 2004, Ryan Webb, out of Clearwater Central Catholic High School.

It's now time for me to try this retirement thing. I want to spend more time with my grandchildren. When I look back, there are a lot of memories. Pinellas is a good county. I've been here practically my whole life, although I was on the road a lot. Selfishly, I wish I could have stayed home a little more. I love the history of Pinellas. I love baseball. Most of all I love my wife, Susan. I am glad to see that this book has captured the essence of Pinellas County baseball and what it has meant—and still means—to a lot of people.

—Tom Kotchman

* Freehan was with the Tigers for fifteen years, retiring in 1976 with a career batting average of .262 and 200 home runs. An outstanding defensive catcher, he was an all-star eleven times and earned five Gold Glove awards. He passed away in 2021.

PREFACE

Pinellas County, Florida, is well known for having hosted spring training for numerous professional baseball teams over the years. Among those setting up camp in St. Petersburg in the past were the New York Yankees, with so many of their greats, including Babe Ruth, Lou Gehrig and Mickey Mantle; the New York Mets of Dwight Gooden, Darryl Strawberry and Tom Seaver; and the St. Louis Cardinals of Bob Gibson and Lou Brock. Still, today, we have the Philadelphia Phillies in Clearwater and the Toronto Blue Jays in Dunedin. And of course, the Tampa Bay Rays have called St. Petersburg their regular season home since joining the American League in 1998.

With the backdrop of the professionals in its backyard, Pinellas County offers another side of baseball lore that needs to be told. This book delves into the baseball people of this part of the West Coast of Florida that encompasses the Tampa Bay area. Readers will recognize some names, but some will be new to them. Some of the people highlighted became major leaguers; some made it to the minor leagues; others starred in high school and college. Some became managers and coaches, scouts or executives. What they all have in common is that they are part of the fabric of Pinellas County one way or another, having either grown up there or lived there for much of their lives. Dozens and dozens of local players, if not many more, have been drafted by major league clubs, clearly making Pinellas County a prime area where baseball dreams can—and have—come true.

Reprints of articles written by author Dan Hirshberg published in the Tampa Bay Weekly Newspaper Group, as well as online at tbnweekly.com, appear in these pages, augmented by a host of never-before-seen individual and team feature stories by Hirshberg. The reprinted articles, some of which have been modified with updates, are noted throughout the book as "originally published," with the date of first publication indicated.

Most readers will recognize many of the people in these pages, such as Casey Kotchman, perhaps the greatest defensive first baseman in major league history; Howard Johnson; Toby Hall; umpire Richie Garcia; and Dewayne Staats, the longtime play-by-play announcer for the Tampa Bay Rays. And then there's Tom Kotchman, Patrick Boyd, Bobby Wilson, Donnie Scott, Boof Bonser, Hank Webb, Todd Vaughan, Greg Olsen, Tom Zimmer, Tim Wilken and Bill Brinker. And yes, many others.

A full chapter is devoted to the memory of Steve Giorgiadis, the Seminole pitcher whose life tragically ended while he was undergoing routine surgery during college. And we highlight three amazing high school championship teams with special stories: 1979 Clearwater Central Catholic High School, 2001 Seminole High School and 2017 Calvary Christian High School.

You don't have to live in or be from Pinellas County, or even have visited Pinellas County, to enjoy reading about the people who make up its unique baseball history. It's all here for the taking. Take a swing and enjoy.

ACKNOWLEDGEMENTS

I could not have done this alone. There are many to thank for their help with this project.

Let's start with Chris George, executive editor of the Tampa Bay Weekly Newspaper Group, who first gave me the opportunity to write about the "baseball people of Pinellas County."

Tom Kotchman has been so helpful over the years. His knowledge of Pinellas County baseball is an encyclopedia of information, and it is no coincidence that you will see his name pop up throughout the book.

Special thanks to everyone who took the time to speak with me about their own careers and others' for this book. A big thank-you to Angela Giorgiadis, whose stories and memories—and timeline details—about her son Steve and his life were truly heart-warming. Greg Olsen at Calvary Christian High School and Adam Moravick at Seminole High School, both current coaches; Todd Vaughan, former coach at Clearwater Central Catholic High School; and Scott Miller, formerly of Seminole High—all went out of their way to provide me with extensive information about their teams. Also a huge shout-out to Beth Lani at Clearwater Central Catholic, who has been a big help with this project and others.

My good friend and colleague Cathy Miller was a gracious—and very patient—photo editor. My daughter Melanie DeStefano provided me with publishing consultation. Longtime friend Jerry Karp gave me excellent editing advice, and Zoe Ames, my copyeditor at The History Press, offered a host of terrific suggestions. My wife, Susan, allows me to pursue my love of writing, whether through this book or the many other projects I am involved with. I am very thankful for that. And a big thanks to my stadium connection, Nate Hirshberg.

I also want to thank acquisitions editor Chad Rhoad of The History Press, who shared my vision for the book and moved it forward.

If I forgot anyone, don't take it personally!

INTRODUCTION

It had been a long time since I'd written about sports on a regular basis, and I found myself, a few years back, hankering to get back into the business. Not full time, not even part time but on a somewhat regular basis, a hobby of sorts more than anything.

In Pinellas County, Florida, baseball runs deep. It is well documented that over the years, the Phillies, Blue Jays, Yankees, Mets and Cardinals (and the Orioles) have all called Pinellas County their spring training home at different times. Add to that the Tampa Bay Rays, the "hometown" team here since 1998, and it dawned on me that many great (and not necessarily so great) players have graced the area. And so I came up with the idea of proposing a baseball column about former players associated with Pinellas County and what they might be up to these days while also reflecting on their playing careers.

In the summer of 2020, I wrote to Chris George, executive editor of the Tampa Bay Weekly Newspaper Group, with this idea in mind. Time passed, and I didn't hear anything back. A month later, when I'd all but given up on the idea, Chris emailed me back. He liked the idea! I was off and running.

My first column featured former Cardinal and longtime team broadcaster Mike Shannon (who passed away in April 2023). I would go on to interview and write about Tony Kubek, Dwight Gooden, Larry Bowa, Davey Johnson, James Shields, Greg Luzinski, original Devil Ray John Flaherty, Howard Johnson, Ed Kranepool (who passed away in September 2024) and others from the pro ranks.

Interviewing and writing about these guys has been a lot of fun. Somewhere along the way, though, I veered deeper into the fabric of Pinellas County baseball and found myself wanting to focus more on those people who either grew up in the area or, in many cases, still lived nearby. This new approach to stories began, in great part, after I interviewed Tom Kotchman, a longtime pro scout and minor league manager. Tom knows everybody, and everybody knows Tom. His knowledge of Pinellas County baseball (and beyond!) is an encyclopedia of the who, what and where of it all. At the time, my own contacts were limited, truth be told. Tom, however, allowed me to tap into his huge network of contacts, and then like a domino effect, one after another, story ideas came bursting to the surface.

As anyone who follows the local baseball scene in Pinellas County knows, there have been many great ballplayers from the high school ranks, and while some have had excellent pro careers, not all of them hit the big-time. To me, it didn't matter if they made it to the Show or not. Their stories were just as enlightening as the other guy's. I also became intrigued by the stories of those who have made a name for themselves connected to baseball in other ways, such as coaches, scouts, umpires, broadcasters, publicists and fans.

This book reflects on what I refer to as the "baseball people" of Pinellas County. Most of the chapters are my original columns. Some may feel there are "baseball names" missing in this book that perhaps should have been included. Maybe they will be part of a second book! In a few cases, it should be noted that I have updated or edited the original articles for this book. Mostly, though, they remain intact, as they were first published.

Everybody has a unique story to tell, and I am glad that I am able to bring some of those stories to life.

CHAPTER 1

TOM KOTCHMAN, A BASEBALL LIFER

Originally published March 31, 2022

When Tom Kotchman made his pro debut with a Cincinnati Reds Class A minor league team in 1977, little did he know that this would be the start of a baseball career that would span over four decades.

Kotchman, a resident of Seminole since 1967, is what they call a baseball lifer. His pro playing career lasted only two years, but his career as a minor league manager, coach and scout endured for years.

After attending Seminole High School and then playing for Chipola Junior College and, later, Georgia Southern University, Kotchman was signed by the Reds in 1977. In two years in their Single-A system, Kotchman put up modest statistics, but by midseason that second year, the writing was on the wall, accentuated by an errant pitch.

"The decision to retire as a player was sort of made for me," recalled Kotchman. "We were playing a game, and there were shadows over home plate. David Palmer was pitching, and it was the fifth inning. He threw me two sliders for strikes, and then he threw one up and in."

Kotchman was hit above the left eye and went down. He ended up needing cosmetic surgery, and when he got back to the team, he was relegated to part-time duty. Instead of brooding about it, Kotchman took advantage of what he could.

"Mike Compton was the manager, and when I was on the bench, I would ask him a lot of questions," said Kotchman. "I coached first base. I made the most out of the situation."

Kotchman, a third baseman, also calculated his long-shot chances of getting to the majors with Cincinnati. "Pete Rose was playing third base for the Reds, and Ray Knight was behind him at Triple-A. But it all worked out for the better."

Tom Kotchman in the on-deck circle at Seminole High School. *Courtesy of Seminole High School.*

Kotchman wasn't out of work for long. In 1979, he got his first managing job—at age twenty-four—when he was picked to pilot the Auburn Redstars in the Class-A New York-Penn League. The next year, he was hired by the Detroit Tigers organization, where he managed for two years; then it was on to the Red Sox for two years.

"For some going from playing to managing, the transition could be hard, but it wasn't for me because I learned a lot from the coaches I played for," Kotchman said.

Many players Kotchman managed would eventually make it to the majors, but one that stood out right away was the Red Sox's first round pick, nineteenth overall, in 1983. The right-handed pitcher who joined Kotchman's Winter Haven team straight out of college was Roger Clemens.

"He came right from the College World Series to us," Kotchman recalled. "He was unbelievable. In the first few games, he struck out thirty-six and didn't walk anybody. I couldn't imagine who could have been drafted before him."

Clemens, who would go on to win 354 games, strike out over 4,500 batters and win seven Cy Young awards, had Kotchman in awe of the pitcher's "total package."

"The way he acted, just a ballplayer and all business," said Kotchman. "No fancy car, no gold chains. And he was in such great shape. He had the strongest legs I ever saw. He ran our other pitchers into the ground."

Years later, Clemens's career was tarnished by steroid allegations, but in 1983, there was none of that. A year after playing for Kotchman, Clemens made his major league debut with Boston.

"As far as what I know of Clemens when he was with me, he was a man among boys," said Kotchman.

In 1984, Kotchman joined the American League's Angels, a tenure that would continue through 2012. In 1990, Kotchman took on a dual role with the club. In addition to manager, he became the team's Florida-based scout. As a scout, he would sign several future Angels, including Howie Kendrick, Scot Shields, Jeff Mathis and two Seminole High School products, Bobby Wilson and Greg Jones.

Kotchman didn't know anything about Shields initially. "I was scouting a player from the University of Western Florida, and they were playing Lincoln Memorial University," he remembered. "Lincoln's pitcher was this skinny, wiry right-hander—six foot one, 160 pounds. I ended up signing him in the thirty-eighth round for $1,000. A few years later, he was on the Angels World Series championship team."

Kendrick, an outfielder, was another player Kotchman had little knowledge about before coming across him in a junior college game. "He was from a small high school, and I had never seen him," said Kotchman. "And then, for crying out loud, later on he becomes a superman in the postseason. As a scout, sometimes you get really surprised."

Kotchman also had a hand in another Angel draft pick: Casey Kotchman. Yes, that would be Tom's son—and someone who had an outstanding major league career as a premier first baseman. Tom speaks highly of not only Casey but also his daughter, Christal, who had a terrific collegiate softball career. "My wife, Susan, and I are very proud of both of them," said Kotchman.

Tom Kotchman and son Casey when Tom was a minor league manager in Edmonton. *Courtesy of Angels Baseball.*

Over his long career in baseball, Kotchman has had the opportunity to meet not just professional baseball players but other professional athletes as well. To that end, he says that along the way, three sports stars in particular made big impressions on him: hockey great Wayne Gretzky, all-star hitter Rod Carew and major league pitcher Jim Abbott, who had the use of only one arm. "All real gentlemen," he said.

There are many who consider Tom Kotchman their version of a real gentleman.

THE SCIENCE OF SCOUTING, ACCORDING TO TOM

Scouting is not as easy as it might seem, Kotchman notes.

"It's not an exact science," he said. "A guy might get four hits in a game, but what were the conditions? So many things go into it. Plus, there is so much information out there with social media. With phones, players can get dissected every day. I try and get through that by determining the character and makeup of the player. I have to trust my eyes."

Kotchman rejoined the Red Sox organization at the end of 2013, where he remained a part of the team until retiring at the end of the 2024 season. He always enjoyed working with young players, even if times had changed somewhat since he started out. Back when he began, there were no cell phones, no internet.

"You have to adapt," Kotchman said, adding that some things stay the same. "You still have to get them off on the right foot. Assume they know nothing. They think they know a lot of things, but they don't. My job was to give them a foundation so that they can go to the next level."

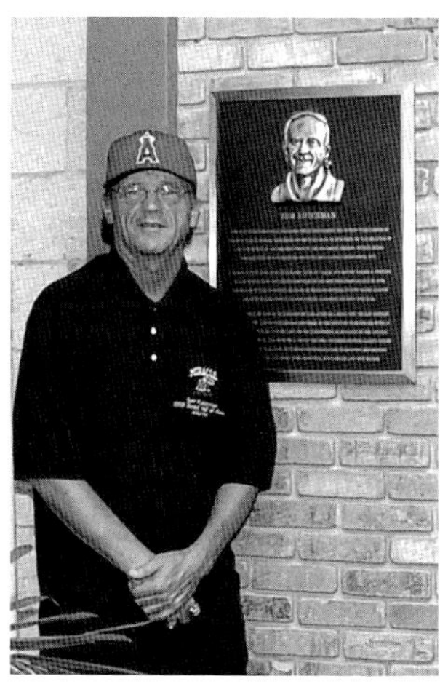

Tom Kotchman was inducted into the Scouts Hall of Fame. *Courtesy of Angels Baseball.*

Kotchman won 2,034 games as a manager, making him thirteenth on the all-time list for minor league skippers (a winning percentage of .546) and, in 2017, was recognized with Baseball America's Tony Gwynn Award for "lasting contributions to baseball."

Kotchman clearly did a great job of creating those foundations, as evidenced by the trust teams placed in him all these years.

Kotchman breaks his success down to an old saying: With youth we learn, with age we understand. "It's a very simple phrase, and that's what I did for forty-some years. I acquired knowledge, and I got it to the kids."

CHAPTER 2

SADAHARU OH STRIKES OUT

Originally published January 27, 2023

How many major league pitchers can say that they struck out Sadaharu Oh, the legendary home run king of Japan? One of the few would be Hank Webb of Tarpon Springs.

Webb was part of a New York Mets postseason goodwill tour to Japan in 1974 when he came face to face with Oh, who cracked 868 homers in his career. Webb, a right-hander who was twenty-four at that time, remembers the punchout pitch well. "It was a slider," he said. "That was definitely a highlight for me."

During the regular season that year—while it might not necessarily have been a highlight for Webb, a late season call-up—his first major league decision came under somewhat rather dubious circumstances on September 11.

"I was on the bench," he recalled. "I was supposed to pitch the next day." At some point, Webb took off parts of his uniform, figuring the game would be over soon. But the game that night against the St. Louis Cardinals went on and on: ten innings, then twenty, then twenty-five. "They told me I had to warm up," said Webb. "I had to get dressed in my full uniform again."

Now it was the early morning hours, and in came Webb in the top of the twenty-fifth. Bake McBride was on first base, and Webb attempted a pickoff throw, but the toss went wild, and McBride came all the way around to score when catcher Ron Hodges couldn't handle the throw home. The Mets went down in the bottom of the inning, so Webb was charged with the loss in what was the National League's longest game ever played to a decision.

Hank Webb once struck out Japanese home run king Sadaharu Oh. *Courtesy of New York Mets.*

"I think it was two thirty in the morning when the game was finally over," said Webb.

The following year, after three seasons of limited major league action, Webb finally got a chance to break into New York's pitching rotation and had his most productive campaign, going 7-6 with an ERA of 4.07 and three complete games and a shutout as the team's fourth starter. He and manager Yogi Berra got along well, and even though the Mets were in the midst of down years after winning the pennant in 1973, Webb was optimistic about the future.

Unfortunately, things didn't work out the next year (Berra was fired midseason). Webb found himself back in the minors for most of 1976 and was traded to the Los Angeles Dodgers at the end of the campaign. He pitched briefly for the Dodgers in 1977, his last season in the majors.

"I played on teams with great pitching staffs, so it was hard for me to stay," Webb said. "The Mets had Seaver, Matlock and Koosman as starters. When I got to the Dodgers, winners of the 1977 National League pennant, they had some good ones, too." The "good ones" included Don Sutton, Tommy John and Rick Rhoden.

"I was very successful in the minor leagues, but I was frozen there," said Webb. "It was difficult to become a starter with the Mets. And later, when I got to the Dodgers, that was a tough staff to try and break into as well. I couldn't really go anywhere. It probably didn't help that I was a little worn down from pitching a lot of innings in the minors. I was hurting."

Webb gave pro ball one more shot in 1978 as a member of the Miami Amigos of the fledgling Inter American League. The team was managed by future Met manager Davey Johnson. The league itself featured around eighteen former major leaguers. But the league folded after one season.

Webb officially retired from baseball after that and got himself into the radio and TV business as an account executive, first with WPLP-570 AM and then what is now known as Fox 13.

While Webb can certainly say he was once a major league baseball player, clearly an accomplishment, his legacy in Pinellas County will always be remembered more for his work as the executive director of Clearwater for Youth (CFY), a job he started in 1985 and ended with his retirement thirty-three years later.

Originally established in 1972, the nonprofit group supports youth athletic programs and other organizations in Pinellas County that emphasize skill-building activities with scholarships, grants and other initiatives. CFY's programs support thousands of children a year.

Webb is proud of the many good things CFY has done over the years: in particular, his efforts in helping to secure fifteen and a half acres of land in Clearwater for what became essentially the organization's home base.

"We basically started with nothing," said Webb. "We added programs, we raised money, we went from supporting a few hundred kids to thousands. We got a building."

If Webb, whose son Ryan was a successful pitcher in the majors for several years, has any ill feelings these days, they're about the fact that major league baseball has essentially locked him out of a pension. He is one of about five hundred former players who fell through the cracks. The plight of Webb and these other players is the topic of a book, *A Bitter Cup of Coffee*, by Douglas Gladstone.

"MLB has ignored this," said Webb.

That sentiment aside, Webb—who grew up on Long Island, New York—mainly has good memories of his ballplaying days. His first interaction with a major league representative was a bit comical, however. "It was 1968, and I was pitching in a CYO game [after the high school season]," remembered Webb. "After the game, Hank Kelly came up to me and said, 'We want to draft you.' I said I had no interest; I was going to Hofstra University. I thought he wanted to draft me into the army! He said, 'I'm with the Mets!' I said, 'Oh yeah, sure!' I signed."

In June 1969, Webb went to rookie ball, where he led his team in ERA and other key categories. He worked his way up the ladder and eventually played in the majors, starting with a late call-up in 1972 and his first major league appearance on September 5.

"It was fun," said Webb. "I was a young guy playing baseball. I got paid seventy-five dollars by Topps and had a baseball card. Ed Kranepool, our first baseman with the Mets, and I used to drive to games together. Bud Harrelson, the Mets shortstop, told me that first year that a ball hit by Roberto Clemente off me was the hardest ball ever hit to him. That's something."

And although he did not play in a World Series, he did play for two teams that won National League pennants, the 1973 Mets and 1977 Dodgers. That's something, too.

CHAPTER 3

TOBY HALL WAS A STEAL

Originally published March 12, 2023

At the Courthouse Performance Center in Oldsmar, former Tampa Bay Devil Ray Toby Hall works with baseball players on every aspect of the game, with one exception. "I kind of do it all," said Hall, "except when it comes to baserunning."

Hall laughs and then explains. "I had zero stolen bases for the longest time," he said. In fact, in a major league career covering nearly eight full years, Hall had all of two steals—and they came in the same game and the same inning!

"We were playing the Yankees in New York right after 9/11 [September 2001], and I was on first base," Hall recalled. "Roger Clemens was pitching, Jorge Posada was the catcher. I thought I saw the third base coach give me the signal to steal. I looked over at the first base coach, and he turned away. So I thought, *Okay, maybe I did get the sign to steal.*"

Hall took off on the next pitch, clearly surprising the Yankees—and his own team—and was safe. And then, a couple of pitches later, Posada threw to second to try and pick off Hall, and Hall took off for third. He got in safely.

"Two stolen bases within four minutes," Hall chuckled. "My next time at bat, Posada looks at me and says, 'Are you kidding me?'"

Later that night, Hall got a call from the front office and was told in no uncertain terms: No more stealing attempts!

Hall, a catcher who played in the majors from 2000 to 2008, mostly with Tampa Bay, these days finds himself "either on a ballfield or at cow shows." He works with baseball players at the Courthouse Performance Center, but he has also spent time traveling with his daughter, Kendall, who shows cows at various events and aspires to become a large animal veterinarian. Toby and his wife, Karra, also have a son, Tayden, who was signed by the Milwaukee Brewers. Like his father, he is a catcher.

Toby Hall was a catcher with the Tampa Bay Rays and has been recognized as a member of their All-Time Team. *Courtesy of Toby Hall.*

Hall proudly notes that at the Performance Center, they've been able to get college scholarships for over one hundred players. "To see that, that's what makes it a lot of fun," said Hall, adding that the center works with about six hundred kids, both in baseball and softball.

What is also fun—and important—for Hall is his relationship with Matthew Walker and the Miracle by the Bay Foundation, an organization that advocates for people with disabilities. Hall's recognition of the challenges of those with disabilities playing sports actually goes back to 2007, when he was with the Chicago White Sox. Around that time, he witnessed a game being played on a Little League field by people with disabilities. That's when he first got to know Walker, who has cerebral palsy. The two kept in touch from then on, and in time, their friendship grew. Walker is the president and chief executive of Miracle by the Bay. "Matt is a real leader," said Hall. "He is amazing."

What eventually came out of that relationship is that the Performance Center has become a partner with the organization and offers an indoor field for their baseball games. "We have the space and are handicapped accessible," said Hall. "This gives them a platform to play here and have some fun. It's really cool to see them succeed."

Players range in age generally from ten to fifty, with a variety of disabilities.

"It's also an eye-opening experience for the kids in our regular program," said Hall. "When they see the people with disabilities and what they go through, it puts an 0-for-4 day in perspective for them."

Hall puts his own major league career into perspective when looking back at his own accomplishments. A career .262 hitter, Hall was better known for his work behind the plate. An excellent fielder, he had a career fielding percentage of .989 and twice had the best fielding percentage at his position

Toby Hall is a supporter of the Miracle by the Bay Foundation. Here, Toby (*standing, in black shirt, second from right*) poses for a "team photo" at the Bay Courthouse Performance Center in Oldsmar. *Courtesy of Toby Hall.*

in the American League in a season. Early in 2023, he was named to the Tampa Bay Rays all-time team at catcher.

"I loved catching," said the six-foot-three Hall, who batted and threw right-handed. "There were a lot of all-star catchers when I played: Pudge Rodriguez, Jason Varitek and Posada. Leading the league two years in fielding, that was pretty good."

Hall was drafted by the Rays before they had a team on the field, in 1997. "I was from California and had never been to Florida," said Hall, who was undaunted about being drafted by an expansion team. "None of that mattered. I just wanted to play major league baseball. Not too many people can say they played in the majors for seven or eight years."

CHAPTER 4

HIS BAT WAS THE TICKET

Originally published December 5, 2021

As a pitcher at Clearwater High School, Howard Johnson put up some pretty impressive numbers, even though his overall won-loss record might not have shown it—impressive enough that between his pitching and hitting, the 1978 graduate caught the attention of the New York Yankees in that year's draft. He was selected by New York in the twenty-third round.

"I loved being on the mound," Johnson said. "It really suited my personality. The ball is in your hand. It's just you competing against the hitter—a great experience."

In his senior year, Johnson was a .500 pitcher with a miniscule ERA in the neighborhood of 1.00 per game. "I had a lot of success—we just didn't knock in enough runs," said Johnson, who had a couple of no-hitters that year. "I remember I lost a few 1–0 games."

Johnson, looking to improve on his stats—and draft position—did not sign with the Yankees, instead opting to attend St. Petersburg Junior College to play on their fall season team, where he pitched and played both the outfield and the infield. In the hitter's box, Johnson got a lot of attention and ended up having an outstanding fall campaign in advance of MLB's winter draft. The Detroit Tigers liked what they saw in Johnson and picked him in the first round of that draft, twelfth overall. Johnson inked a deal, and his major league career was on. The only question left was whether Johnson would be on the mound or in the field.

Howard Johnson speaks after being inducted into the Mets Hall of Fame in 2023. *Courtesy of New York Mets.*

"It was an interesting road," said Johnson, who picked up the nickname HoJo along the way. Finally, minor league manager "Fred Hatfield made it clear that I was only going to be a hitter."

Johnson spent his first two minor league seasons in Single-A with Lakeland, playing both shortstop and third base. "I didn't have the best year in the field the first season," conceded Johnson. "But I worked hard to perfect my defense." The second year he played predominately third base. "I was much improved and had a much better season," he said.

That second season, Johnson also found a consistent groove at the plate, prompting his promotion to Double-A Birmingham, where he whacked twenty-two homers. Over the next couple of years, Johnson played at the Triple-A level but also got some call-ups to the Show. In fact, he started the 1983 Tiger season with the major league club. He would get sent down for more seasoning in May but returned late in the year and finished with a .316 average. The next year was up and down as well.

Helping Johnson get through the highs and lows of those first two years was an older teammate, Enos Cabell. "I guess he liked me, because he would spend a lot of time with me, teaching me about the game and supporting me," said Johnson. "He always seemed to have my back, and I think he even spoke to our manager, Sparky Anderson, on my behalf a few times. He really helped me get through the rough patches."

And then came 1984 and Johnson, sharing time at third base, was in the bigs for good. And what a good year it was, as Detroit won the world championship. Two years later, as a New York Met (he was traded to New York prior to the 1985 season), Johnson played on his second world championship team.

"Being a part of those great teams was amazing," said Johnson. "I really learned a lot from the veterans on both teams. I asked a lot of questions of them, and they helped me be a better pro."

So did Met manager Davey Johnson. "When I came to the Mets, it was almost like a reunion with Davey," said HoJo, again sharing time at third base and shortstop those first couple of years in New York. "I had met him at a baseball camp in Clearwater years before, where he was an instructor. He seemed to look out for me, trying to find ways to use me and give me an opportunity to play and make an impact with the team."

Johnson formed many close relationships during his years with the Mets, which spanned from 1985 to 1993. Two players in particular made the greatest impression on him, including future Hall of Famer Gary Carter. "Gary and I spent a lot of time together," said Johnson. "We lived near each other on Long Island and drove to the ballpark together a lot. We'd talk about baseball and life, and he helped me understand Christianity more. I also had a lot of respect for Keith Hernandez. He played first base and was like an encyclopedia on the field. He knew what to do in any given situation."

Johnson truly came into his own starting in 1987, when he was handed the full-time third base job. He finished the year with 36 homers and 32 stolen bases, his first of three 30-30 seasons.

"Those 30-30 seasons were unbelievable accomplishments," said Johnson. "I am very proud of those seasons. A season is like a marathon, and to be able to do that is not easy."

Johnson's best season ever came in 1991. That year, he won two-thirds of the National League Triple Crown, leading the league in homers with 38 and in RBIs with 117. He also scored 108 runs and had 30 stolen bases. The homers, RBIs and runs scored were all career highs for him. For the second time, Johnson, now an outfielder, was selected to the all-star team.

"I never once thought I could have a season like that," said the switch-hitter, who was coming off a shoulder injury in 1990. "I got off to a really good start and had 63 RBIs at the all-star break, and it kept building throughout the year. The numbers just kept piling up, and I finished it off with a great month of September."

Howard Johnson was honored by the New York Mets in 2023. *Courtesy of New York Mets.*

Johnson played two more seasons with the Mets. His last two seasons were with Colorado and the Chicago Cubs. He retired in 1995. Although not a high average hitter, interestingly, Johnson finished his career with near similar stats for homers and stolen bases: 228 and 231 respectively. In the years since retiring as a player, he has coached in the majors and minors for several teams, including the Tampa Bay Devil Rays for a half-season, and spent two years as a minor-league manager.

While living in Nashville, Johnson helped out at his son Glen's sports facility teaching young people about baseball and what goes into the game. "I've really enjoyed it," Johnson said.

Speaking of Glen, the two did have a truly magic moment in 2011 when Glen was playing for the independent league Rockland Boulders. Dad, then fifty, was invited to play alongside his son for a couple of games during the season. Howard Johnson, with a smile, recalls, "I got myself into playing shape as best I could." In the two games, Glen batted second, and Dad was third.

"Playing with him was really, really cool," said Johnson, who went hitless in the first game and walked in his only at-bat in the second game. "My son was pumped, and it meant a lot to him. Being in the on-deck circle and watching him at bat ahead of me was a great experience"—one of many great experiences, and memories, that HoJo has enjoyed over the years.

CHAPTER 5

FASTBALLS TO SUBMARINES

Originally published September 7, 2022

As a standout baseball player at Gibbs High School in St. Petersburg, Boof Bonser had a well-deserved reputation as a flame-throwing pitcher with an equally outstanding bat. The Pinellas County High School Player of the Year in 2000 had a choice when it came time to turn pro.

"I loved doing pitching and hitting, but I figured the quickest way to get to where I wanted to go in pro baseball was to pitch," the Pinellas Park native said.

Bonser had good reason to think that. By his senior year, he was throwing a fastball around ninety-six to ninety-seven miles per hour while also possessing a nasty hard curve ball.

"It was easy enough to make that decision when you got that kind of velocity, which was unusual for most high school pitchers," said Bonser, a right-hander who finished his senior year 7-3 with an ERA of 1.88 (24-9 and a 1.99 overall in high school).

Bonser, who hit .523 and slammed eleven homers in his senior year, would also play in the 2000 Florida State All-Star game. By then, he had the attention of many pro scouts. In June, the San Francisco Giants grabbed him with the twenty-first overall pick in the first round of the amateur draft. In short order, he made his debut with the Salem-Keizer Volcanoes. Bonser progressed steadily through the minor leagues and, after a trade to the Minnesota Twins organization, eventually made it to the majors in 2006.

Boof Bonser was known as both an outstanding hitter and pitcher in high school. *Courtesy of Minnesota Twins.*

Even before he got to high school, Boof Bonser had an incredible reputation. *Courtesy of Minnesota Twins.*

It was a whirlwind season for the first-year hurler. In his pro debut on May 21, the starter held the Milwaukee Brewers to one run while striking out eight in a no-decision. A week later, he got his first win. In September, Bonser was named the American League Rookie of the Month as he finished the season with a record of 7-6. In October, Bonser started against the Oakland A's in the American League postseason Division Series.

Boof Bonser pitched for the Minnesota Twins for three seasons, 2006–08. *Courtesy of Minnesota Twins.*

"I enjoyed playing in Minnesota," said the six-foot-four Bonser. At one point, he was listed as the team's no. 2 starter.

Bonser would play for Minnesota for three years, earning eighteen wins against twenty-five losses, but his stay there was shortened when he underwent surgery in February 2009 to repair tears in his labrum and rotator cuff and he missed that season. He was then traded to the Boston Red Sox late that year. He saw limited action in Boston and, before the season was over, ended up pitching briefly for Oakland, where he picked up what would be his last major league victory.

Injuries continued to hamper Bonser. He eventually underwent Tommy John surgery in 2011 and, later on, had issues with his elbow. After a few attempts at comebacks, by 2014, Bonser knew it was time to move on.

"Once I had the Tommy John surgery, I really slowed down," admitted Bonser. "I tried to come back. I made a run at it. I was still battling to get through it. Father Time got me, too. I was the older guy, and there were prospects waiting for their turn. Everybody was fair with me. I wish I had more time in the majors, but it didn't work out that way."

Still, Bonser said, "I loved the whole thing. It was what I always wanted to do—play in the big leagues. There wasn't one thing that stands out for me; I enjoyed it all. I even got to pitch in Boston at Fenway Park, with all its history."

One might wonder: If Bonser was starting out now, with strict pitch counts and innings pitched, and more reliance on relief hurlers, would he able to have more success as a starter or a reliever? As far as Bonser is concerned, though, there's no sense in thinking about that.

"It's a different game today," he said. "When I was in the minors, you learned how to pitch one way. Now there are different expectations; you only go so many innings, and you are expected to throw one hundred miles per hour."

Perhaps the biggest mystery about Bonser is: Where did the nickname Boof come from? He was born John Paul. Sometime early on, his mother, Eileen, started calling him Boof. "Growing up, everybody knew me as Boof," he said. "I don't know where that came from, and I don't ask. I leave it at that!"

He legally changed his name to Boof in 2001.

Instead of throwing fastballs, he now helps build submarines for the military in Connecticut. Asked if he wants to share any secrets about the job, he just smiles.

CHAPTER 6

NO SURPRISE, GARCIA'S FIRST EJECTION WAS MARTIN

Originally published April 13, 2023

It didn't take long for Rich Garcia to eject his first manager from a game after becoming a major league umpire. Is it any surprise that it was Billy Martin?

After five years as an umpire in the minor leagues, Garcia was promoted to the majors in 1975, making his debut on April 8 at third base, and he got his first assignment behind the plate a couple of days later. That first series was in Texas, the Rangers hosting the Oakland Athletics. Martin, managing the Rangers, didn't like a call made by Garcia, who was working behind the catcher, on a foul ball dribbler down the third base line.

"He tried to make a big deal of it," said Garcia, who has lived in Clearwater since 1970.

The feisty Martin, being Martin, wouldn't let it go.

"I was a rookie, but I wasn't about to let him intimidate me," said Garcia, who finally ejected Martin. But that wasn't the end of it. Soon after, bench coach Frank Lucchesi kept on Garcia from the dugout. He too, was ejected.

A few minutes later, Ranger batter Dave Nelson told Garcia to "just get behind the plate" because he didn't think things were moving along quickly enough. Bye-bye, Nelson!

For a quarter of a century, from 1975 to 1999, Garcia had a reputation as an outstanding umpire. "A lot of things happened in twenty-five years," Garcia said. "Some good, some bad. You just go with it."

Rich Garcia has plenty of memorabilia from his many years of umpiring. *Courtesy of Rich Garcia.*

There were plenty of "good things," including his participation in five American League Champion Series, four World Series and two All-Star Games. In 1985, Garcia was elevated to American League crew chief. He is one of only seven umpires to work two perfect games: he was behind the plate when Len Barker of the Indians did the trick in 1981, and he was the umpire on second base when David Wells pitched the New York Yankees over the Minnesota Twins in 1998.

On March 31, 1998, Garcia, who has made Pinellas County his home for many years, had the opportunity to work the Tampa Bay Devil Rays' first game at the Trop. He was the home plate umpire for the game against the Detroit Tigers.

Rich Garcia points to himself in a picture from the Tampa Bay Devil Rays' first ever home game in 1998. Garcia was the home plate umpire. *Courtesy of Rich Garcia.*

One of the wildest memories Garcia recalled was the 1989 World Series between the Oakland Athletics and the San Francisco Giants. That Series is best remembered for what happened on October 17. Just before game time, an intense earthquake hit the Bay Area, causing the game to be postponed and putting the Series itself on hold for several days.

"That was crazy," said Garcia, who grew up in Key West, Florida, where earthquakes are unheard of. "I had never been around anything like that in my life. We were ready to go up to the field when it happened. I didn't know what it was. One of the umps with us was from California, and he knew. He said, 'Get under a table.' A little while later, we went out to the field, and my family was out there already [players' and staff's families were brought out onto the field]. I had a lot of family there, a big group. I was very concerned." What everyone found out soon enough is that this was one of the biggest earthquakes in California history, causing major damage to highways and structures and multiple deaths.

Garcia, like any umpire, has had his share of controversial calls over the years. But when it's the postseason, a questionable call can take on a life all its own. That's what happened in Game 1 of the 1996 American League Championship Series between the Yankees and the Baltimore Orioles. With the game tied in the eighth inning, Derek Jeter hit a high fly ball to the wall in right field where Garcia was stationed. Garcia called it a home run. The Orioles immediately argued the call was wrong due to fan interference. Replays indicated that a twelve-year-old fan, Jeffrey Maier, reached over the wall to catch the ball and deny right fielder Tony Tarasco the chance to catch it. The home run ruling stood, and the Yankees would go on to win the game in eleven innings and, eventually, the pennant.

"Replays showed that it was interference, but back then, there were no instant replay challenges," said Garcia. "Yet there are still some questions about it. Had he not stuck his hand out, would it have been a home run or not?"

What bothers Garcia is that the call he made that day counteracts the millions of good calls he made in his career. "A lot of people relate that play to my name," he said, "and don't take into account what I did over twenty-five years."

Garcia's umpiring career came to a sudden end before the start of the 1999 season, when the MLB Umpires Association called for a mass resignation in an effort to get better benefits. The strategy failed, and while many umpires were able to get their jobs back, Garcia was not one of them. He has no regrets about his decision to back the union. "The resignation effort didn't

These days, Rich Garcia spends a lot of time on the golf course. *Author's collection.*

go so well," conceded Garcia. "I won't look back. I felt I needed to be loyal to the union, and I was. They were very, very loyal to us and got us a lot of great things. They helped with the pension and insurance, among other benefits."

Apparently, though, MLB still valued Garcia's knowledge of umpiring. In 2002, he was hired as an umpire supervisor. In 2010, Garcia and his two colleagues Marty Springstead and Jim McKeon were let go under circumstances that are still not fully clear. "They told us they wanted to go into a different direction," Garcia said with some sarcasm.

Umpiring remains in the Garcia family. His son-in-law, Vic Carapazza, married to his daughter Stephanie, has been a highly regarded major league ump for over ten years, and in 2025, he was named a crew chief. Vic wears No. 19, the same number that Garcia wore.

"I've known him since he was fifteen or sixteen years old," said Garcia, who stays active these days playing golf and keeping up with his grandchildren's schedule. "He was always athletic and did very well moving up the ranks."

Garcia, whose friends call him Richie, played ball on the marine corps team in the 1960s. He was also very athletic himself. In his case, becoming an umpire was something of an afterthought.

"I came back home after the service, and I did get some scholarship offers, but I didn't think I had good enough grades to go to college. So I coached baseball at a Catholic school and planned on being a mail carrier with the post office," said Garcia, who has been married to his wife, Sheryl, for fifty years. "One day, a friend of mine who was an umpire locally said he needed someone to help him with a game and would I do it. I told him, 'If I can work the plate, I will do it.' He said no, but I insisted, and he let me do it. I worked that game and loved it. From there, I umpired Little League, Pony League, high school and college games. After one of the games, another ump said I should think about becoming a professional. I looked into it. My first marriage was bad, and I quit the post office job and decided to go to umpire school around 1970. Everybody thought I was nuts. Looking back, I was nuts!"

CHAPTER 7

A MAJOR LEAGUER IN ANOTHER WAY

Originally published August 1, 2024

Patrick Boyd didn't make it to the major leagues as a ballplayer, but in another way, he did make it to the major leagues.

Plagued by injuries throughout his ascent in the minor leagues, Boyd, at one time considered a can't miss switch-hitting outfield prospect who could hit, throw and run, could never quite get into a consistent groove while with the Texas Rangers organization, and as a result, his dream of playing on a major league field fell short.

His climb to the major leagues on another front, however, has been anything but short.

Boyd, who grew up in Palm Harbor and was an outstanding athlete at Clearwater Central Catholic High School, has emerged as a leader in professional baseball's temporary housing industry. As the founder of Pro Housing, Boyd has seen his company go from providing services to one major league team to seventeen these days, offering high-end temporary housing options for their major league and minor league players and staff, with suitable—quality—transitional living arrangements as needed that take away the hassle of locating a rental and dealing with leases.

Boyd left baseball after his last year in the Rangers organization, in 2004, and settled in Scottsdale, Arizona, not far from where the Rangers trained in the spring. He then got into the real estate business flipping houses with his brother. One day, he got a surprise phone call from a Rangers executive.

Patrick Boyd had a good career at Clemson University, highlighted by an outstanding College World Series run in his junior year. *Courtesy of Clemson University.*

"We need someone to set up temporary housing for our players and staff when needed. Can you do it?"

"It started through a relationship and a conversation," said Boyd. "I didn't really know what it was, but I said yes."

Feeling his way through that first year was a challenge. Early on, "I failed," he said with a laugh. "In one case, I forgot to turn off the gas. I got chewed out a lot for four or five days. Somehow, they asked me to do it again the next year. I kept learning more and more. I was learning the business as I was doing everything. I took on a few more teams, and it's grown from there."

In addition to the Rangers, among the many teams Boyd works with now are the Phillies, Mets, Yankees and Pirates. Each team's needs are a little different, but generally, Pro Housing handles housing for not only major leaguers and staff but also their minor league affiliates.

Pro Housing began operations in 2006 and currently has over 1,000 units around the country of varying sizes. The company handles over 7,500 "check-ins" and provides housing for around 1,700 players and staff each year.

The move to more quality housing for professionals has come about in part as a result of the last MLB collective bargaining agreement. This has been particularly a boon to minor leaguers, who once were relegated to sleeping and eating on a shoestring.

"My first year in the minors, I lived with a host family," noted Boyd, who started out in Port Charlotte in 2002 and in the next couple of years played in Savannah; Frisco, Texas; and Stockton, California. "On the road, we were in and out of hotels. When I had a place, you'd have to deal with breaking a lease, and you would get stuck with a lot of late bills. Instead of concentrating on baseball, you had no plan for how to deal with your day-to-day living arrangements—let's put it that way. A lot of peanut butter and jelly sandwiches. You'd eat what you can, maybe leftovers from the concession stands, fast food or food at a gas station."

Patrick Boyd, batting here as a member of the Clemson University baseball team, had a stellar high school career and had incredible potential before injuries took their toll. *Courtesy of Clemson University.*

Boyd's company allows players to concentrate on baseball and also benefits the organizations they play for. "We take all the responsibility: on the lease, turning off the utilities, the bills," said Boyd. "It takes the pressure off the teams, too, knowing players are on a quality bed and getting a good night's sleep, which also allows them to work with the players on nutrition and, most importantly, concentrate on building a winner."

Throughout high school and into college, there was no question that Boyd was a winner. At Clearwater Central Catholic, he was considered one of the region's elite players. He played on clubs that won two district championships, and one of those teams became a regional runner-up. In his senior year, in 1997, Boyd racked up a host of all-star team recognitions while smashing forty-four hits and seven homers, driving in thirty-four runs and setting single-season records for stolen bases (thirty) and runs scored (forty-seven).

Retired legendary CCC baseball coach Todd Vaughan, who worked with dozens of outstanding players over the years, flat-out declared that Boyd was the best. "He was easily the best baseball player I ever coached," said Vaughan. "There was never a debate about that. It was him."

"That was a special place for me," said Boyd, who graduated from high school in 1997. "I had a blast. It was so much fun competing with my team, just a great group of guys. I only wished we could have won a state championship. Really wanted that. Just didn't win it."

Boyd, who was inducted into the school's Hall of Fame in 2023, was drafted by the Seattle Mariners out of high school but chose to go to Clemson University on a scholarship. At Clemson, he continued to impress those around him with his all-around play. In his junior year, when the Tigers made it to the College World Series, Boyd batted .386 with eight extra-base hits in nine NCAA Tournament games. But in his senior year, shortly after he was drafted again, this time by the Pittsburgh Pirates, the first of many injuries to come—a stress fracture to his lower back—cropped up. Boyd's season came to a jarring halt. Still, over his career at Clemson, he amassed terrific numbers. In 191 games, he hit .341 and had 28 home runs, 57 doubles, six triples, 178 RBIs and 49 steals.

Following his senior year, the Texas Rangers were optimistic that the six-foot-three, 205-pound Boyd could rebound from the injury and would be a good investment. They signed him. "I was with the Rangers for three years, 2002–2004," said Boyd. "I was injury-prone. I had a stress fracture that made it tough for me to hit from the right side, and then I tore a ligament in my left hand. I got cortisone shots, and that helped only for a while."

Boyd did have one very good run during the 2003 season while playing with Stockton. In 58 games, he batted. .294, hit 13 homers, drove in 50 and scored 48. He also stole 11 bases.

Unfortunately, the injuries caught up with him, and he realized it was time to move on following the 2004 season. "It has all worked out for me," he said. "Baseball has given me a lot of opportunities. I couldn't be happier about how things have turned out."

CHAPTER 8

DEWAYNE STAATS DESERVES A DAY OFF

Originally published January 2, 2024

For over four decades, Dewayne Staats has called professional baseball games, from the Southwest to the Midwest to the Northeast and Southeast—more than seven thousand contests in all.

So if Staats, the original—and still—the voice of the Tampa Bay Rays, wants to take a day off or two, why not? "I usually take about twenty games off a year," Staats said, during a chat in his Pinellas County condo. "Forty-plus years. The cities and travel aren't as appealing as they once were."

But don't be fooled. While the routine may not be as appealing as when he started out as one of the announcers for the Houston Astros in 1977—and even earlier with the Oklahoma City 89ers—getting behind the mic is still a thrill for the native of Illinois. "I've avoided working and making a living," he said with a laugh.

The baseball season never really ends for Staats. While he winds down somewhat from the long campaign each year, he can't help but keep on top of baseball news during the offseason. "I shut down a little. However, like any fan, I don't want to miss anything," he said in his home office, surrounded by memorabilia, including autographed books and balls. "You never know what you might pick up on and want to refer to during the season. Dick King, who was the 89ers general manager, told me that preparation is 90 percent of the job. That's always stuck with me."

Gene Elston, a broadcast partner with the Astros, was another important figure when it came to game prep during Staats's early career. "He was

Dewayne Staats has been the voice of Tampa Rays baseball since the team began to play in the American League in 1998. *Author's collection.*

meticulous," Staats recalled. "From him, I started keeping detailed statistics daily on pitchers and hitters every game. I put together spiral notebooks with a section for every team. Year to year, you don't know when you'll want to pull information as a frame of reference in a given game." Staats, who has also been a broadcaster over the years with the Chicago Cubs and the New York Yankees, in addition to working with ESPN, still depends on his spiral notebooks.

As a broadcaster, Staats has had the opportunity to call games in stadiums throughout the country. The one stadium, though, that he remembers most fondly is one where he was not an announcer—the original Busch Stadium in St. Louis, previously known as Sportsmen Park. "My father took me to my first game when I was in grade school," said Staats. "We entered Busch, and for me, it was like walking into a different dimension, a different existence. We came up the ramp, and the floodlights were all brilliant. I had never seen grass so green. The colors of the park… It was just the coolest thing for a kid to see."

To this day, he appreciates the old ballparks still in existence. "Wrigley and Fenway, you have to appreciate them," Staats said. "The comfort is not as great as other parks, but with the setting they are in, you put up with that."

Staats was excited years ago when the Baltimore Orioles started the trend of building new stadiums with that old-time feel. "You had a lot of new donut stadiums in the '70s, which may have been comfortable, but they lost their personalities," he said. "Then came Camden Yards. It was great, a real throwback. It is still pretty good to this day."

Staats has garnered numerous memories over the years, starting with his first major league game in the booth, which was actually an audition for the Astros job. The contest was against the Cubs at Wrigley Field and featured a mound matchup between two outstanding hurlers, Houston's J.R. Richard and Chicago's Rick Reuschel.

"I knew it was an audition and a couple of other guys had already tried out," said Staats. "Two amazing things happened that day that helped me get loose and ready. First, Astros broadcaster Bob Prince sat me down and, in his gravelly voice, said to me, 'Don't worry, we'll mess it up together!' And then I ran into Cubs manager Jim Marshall before the game. I knew him from when he was the manager at Wichita when I worked for Oklahoma City. He asked me what I was doing there, and I told him. Well, he took me into his office and gave me a full scouting report on his team, and I was able to use a lot of that information when I was on the air. That was a wonderful act of kindness."

When pressed about his greatest memory, though, Staats doesn't hesitate. It was the last game of the 2011 season, when Evan Longoria hit a home run to beat the Yankees and catapult the Rays into the playoffs as a wild card. It was the culmination of an incredible come-from-behind victory.

"It was so improbable," he said. "It was not so exciting for half the game. Then there were a couple of runs here and there. You're thinking maybe they have a chance to win the game."

Trailing 7–0, the Rays scored six runs in the eighth inning, with Longoria hitting a three-run homer to cap the rally. Dan Johnson homered in the ninth to tie it, and then Longoria cracked the game-winning homer in the bottom of the twelfth to win it. Meanwhile, that day, Baltimore beat the Red Sox, who had been tied with Tampa Bay. The Rays finished 91–71, a game ahead of Boston.

"You had so many possibilities [that day], all the elements," said Staats. "In the end, that was a very exciting game."

Staats counts his lucky stars every day. He has a wonderful wife, Carla; two daughters, Stephanie (who is married to former Ray Dan Wheeler) and Alexandra, both with his first wife, Dee, who passed away after a long battle with cancer; three grandchildren, Gabe, Zach and Evie; and a niece and nephew he and his wife are close to, Sophie and Davis.

"Carla and I were talking the other day about how we look at those five young kids and we realize how fortunate we are to have them in our lives," Staats said. "I've got it good. I love Pinellas. I have been to every state and traveled internationally, but I always love to come back here. I choose to live in Pinellas. It's still the best place to live anywhere."

And then he stepped out onto his patio and looked out over the beautiful waters of the Gulf. "It's been a pretty decent run," he said.

That's putting it mildly.

CHAPTER 9

WHEELER'S GOT GOOD TIMING

Originally published July 13, 2023

Dan Wheeler was called up from the minor leagues to the Tampa Bay Devil Rays during the 1999 season, the team's second in existence, and started a handful of games. That would be a pretty cool thing for any twenty-one-year-old, and it certainly was for Wheeler. Now officially part of the Devil Rays family that offseason, Wheeler was asked to attend one of those caravans around the area to promote the team.

Longtime Rays broadcaster Dewayne Staats was also part of that caravan, and with him at one event was his daughter Stephanie. Wheeler and Stephanie got to talking. "We met at the luncheon, and the rest is history," said Wheeler. He was in the right place at the right time. The two have been married now for over twenty years and have three children, Gabe, Zach and Evie.

Being in the right place at the right time has happened numerous times to Wheeler, who grew up in Rhode Island and has been living in Clearwater for many years. He's played on two World Series teams, threw the last pitch at the old Busch Memorial Stadium in St. Louis that sent the Astros to the World Series in 2005 and has played with many of the greats in the game, including Hall of Famers Wade Boggs and Roger Clemens. When Clearwater Central Catholic High School was looking to hire a new head coach in May 2021, Wheeler was the choice.

"The school has a long history of excellence," said Wheeler, who had previously been an assistant under legendary coach Todd Vaughan. Besides being a good coach, Wheeler says he is "just trying to be the best role model for these kids."

His two sons, first Gabe and then Zach, have played for their father. Is it a little awkward coaching your own sons? Wheeler puts it into perspective. "I remember when Gabe was around nine and I was hard on him after a game," said Wheeler, whose daughter, Evie, took to dance. "I took a step back after that. It's never going to be perfect. You have to enjoy the game."

After a year of junior college ball and then turning down a chance to play for Arizona State, Wheeler was drafted by the Devil Rays in 1996, two years before Tampa Bay officially took a major league field.

"I didn't care that it was an expansion team," said Wheeler. "I figured that if I did something right, I might move through the organization"—and get to the majors quicker. Two and a half years later, he did get to the majors, although it was tough for him to stick with the club for an extended period. "I got a taste, and then I went bouncing back and forth," recalled Wheeler, a starter at first. "You do start doubting yourself."

After three seasons with Tampa Bay, now fully in a relief role, Wheeler got traded to the New York Mets. In 2004, he was shipped to the Houston Astros, the year Houston lost to St. Louis in the National League Championship Series in seven games. "We came really close," he said. "That was an awesome series, even though we lost."

In 2005, Wheeler established himself as one of the top setup hurlers in the game, compiling a 2-3 record with an ERA of 2.21. The Astros got another shot at St. Louis in the NLCS that year, and Wheeler played a pivotal role in the deciding Game 6. With Houston leading 5–1, Wheeler was called on to finish things off in the bottom of the ninth inning. Wheeler quickly struck out Larry Walker and John Mabry for the first two outs. Mark Grudzielanek kept the Cards alive with a line drive single to left. Up to bat came Yadier Molina, always a tough out.

"I got the two Ks, and then that was a ball hit well," remembered Wheeler. "I just said to myself, *Let's get this next guy out*." And he did: Molina hit a harmless fly ball out to right field that ended the game. "That was one of my best moments," admitted the six-foot-three Wheeler. "I was on the mound at old Busch Stadium. That was very cool. And throwing the last pitch that sent us to the World Series."

The Astros, unfortunately, lost to the Chicago White Sox in the Series. However, Wheeler got another shot at a World Series title in 2008 when

Dan Wheeler winds and delivers as a pitcher with the New York Mets. *Courtesy of New York Mets.*

he was once again with Tampa Bay via a midseason trade in 2007. The Rays fell short in their first World Series appearance, though, losing to the Philadelphia Phillies.

Wheeler stayed with Tampa Bay in his second go-round until 2010, putting up some good numbers including thirteen saves, five wins and an ERA of 3.12 during that 2008 season. He finished his thirteen-year career in 2012 with a respectable 3.98 ERA after stops in Boston and Cleveland.

"I was pretty fortunate with the career I had," said Wheeler. "I understand how hard it is to get there. I was lucky enough to play a sport in which I was blessed with a gift to throw a baseball. I wouldn't change a thing. The journey was just amazing. Being a part of major league baseball is a dream. I was lucky to do it."

CHAPTER 10

GOLDEN GLOVE, EVEN IF IT WASN'T

Originally published March 8, 2023

Years before he would become a major league ballplayer, Casey Kotchman got a head start on becoming one of the greatest defensive first basemen in the pros, thanks to his parents, Tom and Sue.

Growing up in Seminole, Kotchman had two pretty darn good "coaches." "I always enjoyed playing catch with Dad and Mom," said Kotchman, whose father was a longtime major league scout and minor league manager.

The back-and-forth of throwing and catching a ball instilled in Kotchman an important lesson. "You can hit .300 and you are considered great, but still, you have failed 70 percent of the time," he said. "But you should be able to catch the ball with a glove every day. That makes for a more complete game."

Kotchman took that "complete game" from his outstanding career at Seminole High School, ranked No. 1 nationally in 2001, to the major leagues. The thirteenth overall pick in the 2001 MLB draft by the Anaheim Angels, Kotchman played in the majors from 2004 until 2013. A good hitter, he was probably better known for his defensive skills at first base.

During a most incredible span, Kotchman went errorless in 274 consecutive games (starting in 2008 and into 2010), handling 2,379 chances flawlessly as a member of the Angels, Atlanta Braves, Boston Red Sox and Seattle Mariners. "I had no idea that I was breaking any records until, at some point, somebody told me," said Kotchman.

Casey Kotchman first showed off his outstanding fielding skills at first base with Seminole High School. *Courtesy of Seminole High School.*

Those records are in the Guinness Book of World Records, and the game streak is also ranked No. 8 on the Bleacher Report's list of baseball streaks that may never be broken. The Bleacher Report put Kotchman's record ahead of others set by names like Barry Bonds, Carl Hubbel, Cy Young, Mariano Rivera and Lou Brock. Admitting he was not aware of the Guinness and Bleacher Report designations, Kotchman humbly offered, "I don't know if I agree with that assessment."

Now here's the crazy rub about the records and Kotchman's overall career fielding percentage of .998: despite his stellar play at first base, he never won a Gold Glove.

"I never won a Gold Glove, but I did get not one but two bases presented to me," he said with a laugh. "I wasn't really surprised that I didn't get a Gold Glove during the streak since I was getting shipped around the country, changing costumes and switching leagues during that time. That's how some things work."

There was no changing of "costumes" in Kotchman's early years in the majors. After three years of splitting time in the minors and majors, and overcoming mononucleosis in 2006, the left-handed hitting and fielding Kotchman became the Angels' starting first baseman in 2007. He started the season with a bang, smashing a home run in his first at-bat. Kotchman finished with a .296 batting average. He might have hit better for the season, but a concussion he suffered on the base paths in June, at a time when he was batting .333, clearly had an effect. Still, Kotchman had one of his best seasons, which culminated in one of six postseasons that he was able to participate in.

Kotchman was feeling pretty good and was off to another solid start in 2008 when, about two-thirds of the way into the season, he was traded to Atlanta. "We were in first place by eleven and a half games when I was traded," said Kotchman. "My team was in the lead, and then I was traded. It certainly gets you out of your comfort level. It breaks your momentum."

The next year, Atlanta swapped him to Boston. Then came Seattle in 2010. "It's like a merry-go-round," Kotchman said. "It gets difficult to get comfortable."

And then he came home. The Tampa Bay Rays signed Kotchman to a minor league deal, and that's where he started the 2011 season. A few games into the season, Manny Ramirez retired, and Kotchman got the call to come to St. Pete. He made the most of it, hitting a career high .306 with ten homers.

"I was really excited to come to the Rays," he said. "I was actually hoping that they would draft me out of high school. I was hoping to stay close to home. I like it here."

At the end of the year, Kotchman was ready to re-sign. "I kept hearing that they were thinking of bringing me back, that there was a good chance, but they never did make me an offer," said Kotchman, still puzzled. "It wouldn't have taken that much to sign me."

Instead, Kotchman signed with the Cleveland Indians, where he had a pretty decent season as the everyday first baseman. But again, no offer came at the end of the season. Kotchman finally signed a deal with the Miami Marlins, where he made the opening day roster. He never got into a groove, though, and popped a hamstring shortly into the campaign. A few months later, he was released, and although he tried to latch onto the Kansas City Royals and the Toronto Blue Jays, neither worked out.

Top: Casey Kotchman takes the field for the Los Angeles Angels. *Courtesy of Angels Baseball.*

Bottom: Casey Kotchman at bat for the Los Angeles Angels. *Courtesy of Angels Baseball.*

"I never really retired; I got retired," said Kotchman. "It's not like I walked away. I just wasn't able to get a job."

Though the career ending wasn't the best, there was good that came out of it later on. His former Cleveland teammate Travis Hafner, who had joined the Yankees and was training in Tampa, introduced Casey to his future wife, Abby.

When asked if he gets any pangs about baseball during spring training, he simply responds with a question, "What time of year is it? I'm just taking it day to day and having fun with my family."

CHAPTER 11

CLEARWATER CENTRAL CATHOLIC PUT ON THE MILES IN 1979

If there ever seemed to be a high school baseball team that was destined to be a state champion, it's probably not Clearwater Central Catholic in 1979.

The Marauders did well during the regular season, but not great. With a regular season record of 14-6 (and a tie), nobody expected Clearwater Central Catholic to do very much in the state playoffs.

"We started slow, but then we caught fire," said the head coach at the time, Bill Gasper. When the playoffs rolled around, CCC played like a team possessed. The Marauders didn't have any power hitters, relied mainly on two pitchers, were forced to travel more than a thousand miles over the course of a few days and had to come from behind several times before claiming the Florida 2A championship title.

What the Marauders did have was a senior-dominated team, a bunch of solid contact hitters and two of the gutsiest pitchers on the mound. "We had experience and unity," remembered former longtime CCC baseball coach Todd Vaughan, the shortstop on that team. "A lot of us had been playing together for a while." That team featured nine seniors: Vaughan, Kevin Kisz, Greg Burhman, Jay Collins, Todd Kovach, Jerry Smith, Jay Collins, Brian Shriver and Mark Mucci.

That experience and unity clearly paid off once the playoffs started, even if the first game nearly derailed the squad's dream of a title. CCC drew Admiral Farragut in the division kickoff. It was looking pretty easy after three and a half innings, CCC on top 7–0. Several starters came out with the win in sight, but then Admiral Farragut battled back. Suddenly, the Marauders

(Standing) Scott Ranier, Coach Gasper, Jay Collins, Greg Burhman, Craig Gilman, Stat girl Nancy Butler, Asst. Coach Grantham, Mike Ficcarotta, Mark Davis. (Kneeling) Mark Araujo, Elliot Mallard, Kevin Kisz, Todd Kovach, Doug Swan. (Sitting on ground) Todd Vaughn, Jerry Smith, Ron Bianco, Mark Mucci, Brian Shriver, Tom Guckian, Glenn Kovach.

Above: The 1979 Clearwater Central Catholic High School baseball team poses for a laid-back team photo. *Courtesy of Clearwater Central Catholic High School.*

Left: Todd Vaughan (*left*) listens as coach Rod Gasper offers advice. *Courtesy of Clearwater Central Catholic High School.*

were behind 8–7. Taking advantage of the reentry rule, the starters came back in for the sixth inning, and CCC scored three runs in the seventh for a 10–8 win.

After the Marauders beat Santa Fe, 4–0, to win the district title, it was on to the regional championship round against Avon Park, a school that had beaten CCC in the regional championship the year before. With the weather playing havoc, things got a lot crazier the rest of the way.

The Avon Park game was scheduled for a Tuesday, but rain forced the contest to be rescheduled for Thursday morning. The Marauders squeaked by, 2–1, to get their payback over Avon Park.

In the sectional final at Umatilla, slated for the next day, Friday, more rain came, and the game was called after one inning. It was then rescheduled for Saturday, which meant the Marauders had to get on the bus, head back to Clearwater and then return the very next day. Of more concern, the overloaded schedule due to the rainouts was stretching out their two main pitchers, Jay Collins and Elliot Mallard. None of that mattered on Saturday because CCC toppled Umatilla, 6–1, to take the sectional championship.

A highlight of the victory was a first inning home run by Craig Gilman. The long drive caused some controversy. "The ball hit a cow grazing in the pasture out there," Gasper recalled with a laugh. "Some of the fans didn't appreciate that."

Now, CCC, which was looking to win the school's second state championship (the first was in 1971), set its sights on the big prize: another state championship.

The state finals were scheduled at the University of Florida in Gainesville, which meant at least one, or two, long round-trip bus rides to the college baseball stadium. In the semifinal, CCC knocked off the defending state champs, John Carroll High School, the difference a two-run single off the bat of Kisz to drive in a pair of runs. The victory set up a showdown with Newberry High School for the championship. After falling behind 1–0, the Marauders again came from behind and overtook Newberry to win 6–3. The final out came when Vaughan went deep into the hole at short to grab a grounder and force the runner out at third base. The incredible—some might say improbable—postseason run was a storybook finish as Clearwater Central Catholic capped the season with a record of 20-6.

The big victory celebration did not come right away. After beating Newberry, the team stopped for food near the stadium before continuing down the road. The yellow school bus, which had rolled up way too much mileage in the last few days, broke down that night near Wildwood. It would be several hours before another bus could be dispatched from CCC to gather up the players for the trip home.

"We were in the dark waiting," said Vaughan. "Not much to do. That was our celebration! Jay Collins broke it up at one point. He said, 'Well, I suppose we could've lost.'" The team eventually made it home at about three o'clock in the morning. A few hearty fans were waiting for them, which "made us feel special," said Gasper.

The title was surely a team effort, with many contributors during the season. The Marauders had five .300 hitters, led by the left fielder, Shriver, at .338 and followed by junior catcher Scott Ranier, .333; Gilman, a sophomore third baseman, .329; Kovach, .320; and, also cracking the .300 mark, Burhman, the first baseman. Other team members included Mike Ficcarotta, Mark Davis, Mark Araujo, Doug Swan, Ron Bianco and Tom Guckian. Les Grantham was the assistant coach.

"We had a lot of catalysts in the lineup," said Vaughan, known for his outstanding defense. "We were a fast team."

In many ways, though, the pitchers Collins and Mallard made the difference. Collins, the school's quarterback, hadn't played baseball the year before. "He came back for his senior year and was our best pitcher," said Vaughan. "Not sure how we would have done without Jay."

"Jay and Elliot were both workhorses," added Gasper. "We had games Monday, Wednesday and Friday, and I'd switch them every other day."

Vaughan remembered that "several times Collins was quoted in newspaper articles as saying that his arm hurt, that his arm was killing him, but that he thought he could hang in there." Collins certainly did hang in there, and so did the 1979 Clearwater Central Catholic Marauders.

Jay Collins was a workhorse pitcher for the 1979 Clearwater Central Catholic High School state championship team. *Courtesy of Clearwater Central Catholic High School.*

CHAPTER 12

GARTON SPOILS A-ROD'S FINAL AT-BAT

Originally published February 16, 2024

It was August 12, 2016, and Tampa Bay Rays rookie right-hander Ryan Garton was on the mound in the bottom of the seventh inning at boisterous Yankee Stadium. The crowd of 46,459 got even louder as Alex Rodriguez stepped up to the batter's box for his fourth at-bat of the evening. Garton didn't realize it, but this was to be A-Rod's final time at the plate. A few days later, he officially retired.

With the fans roaring, hoping for one last big home run swing from the veteran slugger, Garton quickly silenced the crowd.

Garton, who was born in Clearwater and lived in Palm Harbor until the fourth grade before moving with his family to New Port Richey, did not hesitate when asked about the memory. "A first pitch cutter," he quickly recalled.

Rodriguez, who earlier in the game had a double against starter Chris Archer, swung at the pitch and grounded out to shortstop to disappoint the fans—but not Garton. "When I got back to the dugout, someone told me, 'Hey, that was Rodriguez's last at-bat,'" said Garton, who pitched the last two innings in that game. "I still have the picture of that." It's a great memory for someone who admits that if he was looking to break into the majors these days, it would be a lot tougher.

Garton was selected by the Rays in the thirty-fourth round of the major league baseball draft in 2012 after a successful run at Florida Atlantic University, where he focused on pitching after initially being a two-way

Ryan Garton fires a pitch for Florida Atlantic University. *Courtesy of Florida Atlantic University.*

player. Not long afterward, baseball dropped the later rounds. These days, the draft only lasts twenty rounds.

"I might not even have been drafted today, with the shorter rounds," he said. Plus, added the five-foot-ten Garton, "I'm not the physical specimen they're looking for in a pitcher nowadays. I'm not six-foot-five, and I don't throw one hundred miles per hour."

All that aside, the Rays at the time clearly saw something in Garton, who was 21-11 over four years at FAU when they drafted him. "I am thankful for the Rays," he said. "I got an unbelievable chance to make the majors."

Longtime FAU baseball coach John McCormack was always impressed with Garton's work ethic and felt confident that he had the tools to make it. "He worked and worked and made himself a great pitcher for us," said McCormack. "He did the same thing in pro ball. He outworked guys and made it to the big leagues. I am very proud of him and his accomplishments."

It would take a few years, but finally, on May 25, 2016, Garton was promoted to the major league club. The next day, he made his pro debut in a relief role against the Florida Marlins at the Trop. "Getting called up, that was huge," said Garton. "That was cool. Pitching against the Marlins, I did well the first inning, not so hot the second inning."

In fairness, it was a not-so-good game for the Rays overall: they lost 9–1. A few days later, on Memorial Day, Garton pitched in a packed house at Kaufmann Stadium in Kansas City. He felt like that was his first real introduction to the major leagues and all its hoopla. "It was amazing," he said. "Sellout crowd, [plane] flyovers before the game: very American, very intense."

In all, Garton was a reliever in thirty-seven games in 2016, finishing with a win and two losses and also capturing his one career save on July 4 against the Angels, highlighted by a big punch-out against Mike Trout, caught looking at a third strike.

Garton started the 2017 season with Tampa Bay and was traded to the Seattle Mariners in August. After a year back in the minors, Garton briefly pitched for Seattle in 2019. After signing with the Minnesota Twins in November 2019, Garton was looking forward to the 2020 season, but COVID-19 didn't help, and soon after, his major league career ended.

"I was fortunate for my time in the majors," said Garton. "I pushed my body to its limits. I was fortunate to play as much as I did. I was a pro for ten years—I'm happy with it. It was a dream, a goal. It's not like the real world. You can never get the same satisfaction out of another job. As my wife, Christina, reminds me, not everybody gets to chase the dream and accomplish what I did."

Garton probably could have extended his pro baseball career in another capacity, but that did not appeal to him. "I could have gone a different route as a coach in the minors," he said. "I spent a lot of time in the minors, though, as a player, and while some guys can do it, it's not easy with a wife and family. It wasn't for me."

CHAPTER 13

A CATCH FOR THE RANGERS

Originally published October 6, 2021

Bobby Wilson has lived in a lot of places in his life, thanks to a major league baseball career that has taken him to California, Arizona, Texas, Minnesota and Michigan. If you count stops in the minor leagues, you can add places like Utah, Pennsylvania and Oklahoma. So even though the former catcher could have settled down in any of those locales, some more exotic than others, when all's said and done, there's only one place Wilson wants to call home. And that's Pinellas County.

"I'll never leave here," said Wilson, the catching coordinator for the Texas Rangers. "I was born and raised here. I love it here." Wilson also has a professional tie to the area: he once played with the hometown Tampa Bay Rays.

Wilson was part of Seminole High School's incredible 2001 championship season, when it went undefeated and was ranked No. 1 in the country. Wilson, who has three daughters with his wife, Lori, remains close with several of his high school teammates. "The group of guys I grew up with had success on all levels, from Little League and traveling teams to high school," said Wilson. "I am still friends with them. They're a very special group of guys. They'd still do anything for you. It's very cool."

The culmination of their success together was the 2001 team that went 31-0 and won the state championship (even though they had to forfeit a few early season games due to an ineligible player). Wilson, one of the leaders on that club, was recognized as the regional Player of Year at the end of that campaign.

"We were blessed with a lot of people also coaching us, parents with pro experience," said Wilson, mentioning Tom Kotchman as an example. Kotchman's son Casey, who would become a first-round draft pick, was a teammate of Wilson's. Tom Kotchman had been a scout and minor league manager for more than forty-five years.

Wilson thought he might be a high draft pick as well, but that didn't happen. Instead, he turned his attention to the University of Mississippi, which seemed like it "would be a good fit."

Unfortunately, that didn't work out due to finances. St. Petersburg Junior College got wind of Wilson's situation and offered him a full ride, and that's where he played for two years. After a so-so freshman year, the San Francisco Giants drafted him in the twenty-fourth round. Wilson decided to stay at St. Petersburg to see if he could improve on his numbers and, ultimately, be a higher draft pick. That decision would pay off for him: he excelled in his second year, eventually being named a Florida College Player of the Year.

And here's where Tom Kotchman came up big again for Wilson. Kotchman, managing in the Los Angeles Angels farm system, pushed the team to draft and sign Wilson. "I owe a lot to him," said Wilson. "He taught me a lot of things: about being a professional, about being a man."

It took a few years, as it typically does for players going through the minor league system, before Wilson got the call he'd been waiting for since he was a kid. It came in 2008, when he was playing for the Angels' Triple-A team, the Salt Lake Bees. He'd gotten off to a sensational start with the Bees, hitting .339 and driving in twelve runs in just sixteen games.

"I really wasn't expecting it," admitted Wilson, who got the nod on April 28. "It was early in the season." Wilson might have heard the good news a little earlier, except his cell phone wasn't working. Nobody could get ahold of him. At the time, he was living with four or five guys, and eventually one of the other players was contacted and told to get Wilson's attention. "It was about 2:00 a.m. when he told me about the call," said Wilson. "I got the phone back working and saw that there were a lot of missed calls and voicemails."

Later that day, Wilson was wearing an Angels uniform and was inserted into a game against the Oakland Athletics as a defensive replacement. Shortly thereafter, he got his first major league at-bat and hit a single off Dallas Braden. Wilson laughed, "I was sent back down to the minors pretty quick without another at-bat, so I led the majors with a 1000 batting average for the next four months" before he rejoined the team later in the season.

Wilson was up and down over the next year but pretty much became a mainstay on the major league roster starting in 2010 and into 2011.

In April 2010, Wilson's career came to a screeching halt for about two months after he was involved in a head-on collision with the New York Yankees' Mark Teixeira, who was looking to score on a hit. Wilson was knocked away and suffered a broken ankle and a concussion. "He had intentions besides trying to score," Wilson asserted. "He had room to slide without hitting me. I felt the effects of that for a while." Wilson says he doesn't have any hard feelings about the incident anymore and that he and Teixeira have been friendly since.

If that game was Wilson's toughest on the field, a year later, he more than made up for it with what he deems "the highlight of my career." Typically, Wilson was behind the plate for either a travel day (usually when the team left right after a game for the next series) or a day game. On July 27, 2011, it was both, and he was to be the catcher for ace Ervin Santana in a game in Cleveland against the Indians. "It was a hot day. The sun was beating down on me," Wilson remembered. "It was really crushing hot."

While things didn't start out so well for the team, the end result was amazing: Santana struck out ten en route to a no-hitter, the first for an Angel in twenty-seven years.

Leadoff batter Ezequiel Carrera was safe on first after shortstop Erick Aybar was charged with an error. Carrera stole second and moved to third on a ground out. Seconds later, he scored on a wild pitch. That would turn out to be the Indians' only highlight of the game. By the ninth inning, with the Angels in front 3–1, the pressure was building.

"Up until the ninth, we were just trying to win," said Wilson. "In the ninth inning, we started to feel it, and Ervin finished it off." There was a mass celebration on the field—and a very happy party on the plane ride later on.

Santana remains a lifelong friend of Wilson's. "He's a special guy," said Wilson. "He gave me a really nice watch after the game. I still wear it pretty much every day."

Wilson's ten-year major league career eventually took him from the Angels to a few other teams, including the Tampa Bay Rays on two occasions. His first stop with the Rays in 2015 was tougher than he expected as friends wanted his attention now that he was back home. The second time, a year later (with stops in between elsewhere), it worked out better.

"Coming home after twelve years the first time was rough, and I didn't play well," Wilson admitted. "The second time I told my dad [Bobby Sr.]: 'You take care of everybody and tickets.' I was able to focus more on just playing."

Bobby Wilson is a key member of the Texas Rangers coaching staff. *Courtesy of Texas Rangers.*

While Wilson's major league career stats may not have been earth-shattering, he clearly earned a reputation over the years as somebody teams could count on when needed. Three of the teams he played for had enough confidence in him to bring him back for a second go-round. That reputation brought him to his current job with the Rangers, whom he played for twice. He was hired as the catching coordinator in October 2020 after a year as a manager in their farm system. In this capacity, he travels with the team and keeps in contact with catchers in the farm system to make sure everybody's techniques and "standards" are spot-on and aligned with what the club expects.

Wilson summed up his baseball career this way: "I've always been able to grind it out."

CHAPTER 14

NOT ALL ABOUT WINS AND LOSSES

Originally published October 18, 2023

There is no denying that Clearwater Central Catholic's legendary coach, Todd Vaughan, put up some incredible numbers during a storied thirty-three-year career at the helm. For starters, a record of 578-287, two state titles, eighteen postseason playoff runs and seven teams that made it to the Final Four. And then there's the numerous players he coached who went on to success in college and in the pros.

No doubt when the *Tampa Bay Times*, a few years back, ranked him twenty-seventh among the top fifty greatest coaches in the Bay Area of all time, it was well deserved. To Vaughan though, it wasn't always winning big that made for great teams. "Some of the best teams I had didn't go to the states," said Vaughan, who retired in 2021. "But what they accomplished at their level was just as great as some of my other teams."

Vaughan pointed to one of his teams that started the season 2-9 but went on to finish 19-11. "They found it at the midpoint of the season and took off," said Vaughan. "They bought into what we were about and turned it around. Man, what they accomplished."

Most of Vaughan's seasons were successful, of course, but he added, "Rebuilding can be fun, too." He said a lot of that success had to do with his assistants and the players themselves. "I always had real good assistant coaches; I was blessed that way," he said. "I made sure they had a voice, and that was also how it was with the players. I tried to show them the path, and I relied on the kids to make good decisions on their own. You know, they

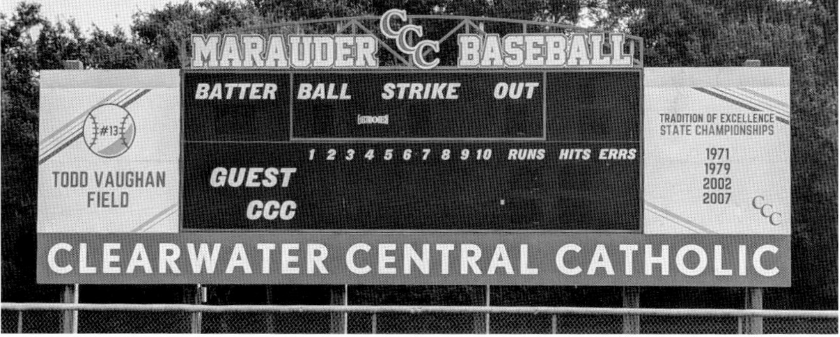

Top, left: Todd Vaughan as a senior at Clearwater Central Catholic High School. *Courtesy of Clearwater Central Catholic High School.*

Top, right: The Clearwater Central Catholic baseball field was renamed Todd Vaughan Field in 2022. *Courtesy of Clearwater Central Catholic High School.*

Bottom: Clearwater Central Catholic's scoreboard at Todd Vaughan Field highlights the school's four state championships. *Author's collection.*

came in at fourteen or fifteen and left a man at eighteen. That's a whole lot of growth in between."

Some of the players who have—or had—ties to major league teams and played for Vaughan include Shawn Williams, who was a minor league manager with the Philadelphia Phillies, and Ryan Weber and Ryan Webb, both of whom have pitched in the majors. "That's kind of neat seeing guys coaching or on television," said Vaughan, who was the shortstop on Clearwater Central Catholic's 1979 state championship team.

Vaughan has seen plenty of great ones come through his program, but he doesn't hesitate when talking about one guy in particular: Patrick Boyd. Boyd, who graduated from CCC in 1997 and, in 2023, was inducted into

Todd Vaughan was inducted into the Clearwater Central Catholic High School Athletic Hall of Fame in 2004. He poses here with two of his former players, Ryan Webb (*left*) and Ryan Weber (*center*), both of whom pitched in the major leagues and were inducted into the school's Athletic Hall of Fame in 2017. *Courtesy of Clearwater Central Catholic High School.*

the school's Hall of Fame, was a six-foot-three, 205-pound outfielder and a USA All-American. He went on to play for Clemson University and, later, was in the Texas Rangers organization for four years. "He was easily the best baseball player I ever coached," Vaughan said. "There was never a debate about that. It was him. We had a whole bunch of guys over the years."

Vaughn also mentioned others, including Chris Hart, Blake Wright and pitcher Gary Wilson. In 1991, in the state tournament, Wilson started a game against a team featuring Alex Rodriquez.

Vaughan, who lives in Clearwater, has had plenty of time to reflect on his coaching career. "All the time I was there, I enjoyed all of it," he said. "Just being around the players and feeling like I did it the right way and with a high academic standard."

The school inducted Vaughan into its Athletic Hall of Fame in 2004 and, in 2022, named its baseball field after him: Todd Vaughan Field.

Does he miss coaching? "There are parts I miss and parts I don't miss," admitted Vaughan, who was replaced as head coach by former major leaguer Dan Wheeler. "I missed my kids growing up. And I have grandkids growing up now, and I don't want to miss being there with them. That's the most important thing to me right now."

CHAPTER 15

A LIFE CUT WAY TOO SHORT

It was April 29, 1988, and Steve Georgiadis was pitching the game of his life against Clearwater in the Class 4A District 7 tournament final. It was clear from the start that the left-hander had something special that day in a year that was already extra special for the Seminole High School pitcher.

When the action was over after seven innings and the Warhawks had won the district championship by a score of 6–1, Georgiadis had struck out nineteen batters, five times striking out the side. He gave up one run on six singles and yielded no walks: he was pretty much untouchable. His only real threat came in the sixth inning when Clearwater loaded the bases. Coach Bill Brinker had faith in Georgiadis, though, and the senior hurler came through with a strikeout and ground out to end the late-game rally. That was it for Clearwater. Georgiadis finished his performance with a flurry, striking out the side in the seventh inning.

If the pitching heroics weren't enough, Georgiadis whacked an opposite field three-run homer in the third inning to help spark the offense. The win gave Georgiadis his twelfth victory of the season.

In his last game on the mound that year, the six-foot-two Georgiadis struck out another ten batters, but the Warhawk bats fell silent in a 3–0 loss to Sarasota in the Regions.

But what a season! Georgiadis finished his senior year with a 12-3 record (most wins in Pinellas County), striking out 129 hitters in 92 innings, issuing only 25 walks and fashioning a miniscule ERA of 1.14. He was a No. 1 selection on several postseason all-area teams, including those picked by

Left: Lefthander Steve Giorgiadis goes into his windup. *Courtesy of Seminole High School.*

Right: Seminole High School batterymates pitcher Steve Giorgiadis (*right*) and catcher Barry Sullivan. *Courtesy of Seminole High School.*

local newspapers. Georgiadis was excited for his next stop on the ballfield: he had a scholarship ticket to attend the University of Florida in the fall.

"I had some good pitchers; he was one of my best," said Georgiadis's coach at Seminole, Bill Brinker, who retired years ago. "Maybe the best that I had. I wish I could have had a dozen players like him."

"He threw strikes and could throw in the mid- to late '80s," noted former major league baseball scout Tim Wilken. "He was extremely reliable."

Longtime MLB scout and minor league manager Tom Kotchman of Seminole added, "He could locate it! He would strike out fifteen and not walk anybody. If you scored a run, you had a good chance to win."

Some thought Georgiadis may have had the tools to go further, even beyond college. Montreal Expos pitching coach Larry Bearnarth befriended and worked with the teenager for about five years during the offseason, and Georgiadis took all that advice to heart in making himself a better hurler.

Everything was looking up for Georgiadis when he got to the University of Florida. The freshman got off to a decent start and had a record of 2-2 with a boatload of strikeouts before shoulder problems started to develop late that first season. In the summer, though, Georgiadis went to Missouri to play in a college league. On his return, the shoulder issues continued. There was some speculation that Georgiadis's arm was overused in Missouri, which probably did not help. As the problems persisted, rotator cuff surgery ensued in the fall of 1989 and then physical rehabilitation. Finally, in the late winter of 1989, it was time to test the arm again. It did not go well, and now a second, seemingly routine, surgery was recommended to take care of some apparent ligament issues. In mid-March 1990, Georgiadis went under the knife once more, with high hopes and an expected full recovery.

The surgery went well. Then, during the recovery over the next couple of hours, something went way wrong, and Georgiadis suddenly—shockingly—died. The nineteen-year old had been vomiting, and it is believed that while he was in a deep sleep, that may have played a role in his death.

Angela Giorgiadis took this photo of her son, Steve Giorgiadis, when he was a Florida Gator. *Courtesy of Angela Giorgiadis.*

Steve Giorgiadis spent a summer pitching in the Midwest. He is pictured here with his host family and his mother, Angela, on the left. *Courtesy of Angela Giorgiadis.*

Steve Giorgiadis (*back row, third from left*) with his 1998 teammates. *Courtesy of Seminole High School.*

"That was really tough," remembered Brinker. "Everybody on the team loved him. He was a good young man."

Although Georgiadis didn't go out for the Seminole High School baseball team right away, he turned out to be one heck of a good young pitcher for the Warhawks. He didn't go out for the Warhawks baseball team in his first year mainly for one reason, according to his mother, Angela. His family moved from Brooklyn, New York, to Florida when he was twelve. The school systems had different starting age requirements, so Georgiadis may have been in the same grade as his classmates in Florida, but he was a year younger. That first year, "he didn't want to go out," said Angela. "He was intimidated by the older boys, and he felt that he wouldn't be good enough."

Georgiadis did continue to play American Legion ball, and the next time around, he was ready to compete for a spot on the high school team. "I kept telling Brinker, 'I got a good player for you,'" said Angela, who was working as a volunteer at the time with the school's athletic department and athletic director Chuck Toohey and would see Brinker in the hallways. He said, 'Let's see.'"

Soon enough, Brinker was impressed with what he saw, and eventually, that culminated in that fantastic senior season. Steve's biggest fan was his mom. Angela would go to every game and even became a big part of the team's pregame procedure. "Steve always wanted my spaghetti and homemade meat sauce before every game," she recalled. "Ballplayers are very superstitious. After a while, I was making spaghetti for some of the other players, and even Coach Brinker asked Steve to bring him some."

What makes Angela most proud of her son was how he was very respectful of others, on the field and off. "He wasn't cocky," she said. "That was one of his greatest traits. He always kept his cool. He didn't throw his glove down. He was always very nice to people."

And he loved to help people. "One of his teachers asked him if he would coach her son," remembered Angela. "He did that on Saturdays. It was like an honor for him to do that rather than a chore." Steve would also spend most of his after-school hours at the baseball field, helping Coach Brinker.

For the family, a huge reason for the move to Florida was recognizing Steve's love—and potential—for the game of baseball. "That was one of the reasons we moved to Florida," said Angela. "By the time he was ten, it was evident that he had a passion for baseball. He played Little League in Bay Ridge, Brooklyn, and he showed a lot of promise. He was turning out to be a good pitcher. Steve was always thinking about baseball. He practiced pitching in front of a mirror. We had a long living room, and he would run and practice his sliding into the dining room."

Steve's team won a championship, and during the team's pizza party celebration afterward, actor Tony Danza came by and joined in on the festivities. But baseball in the north only happens a few months out of the year due to the weather.

The family, which included Steve's dad, Stratos, and younger sister, Christina, made the tough decision to pick up stakes and move south, where they opened up a family restaurant. "I didn't want to leave," said Angela. "I grew up in New York. But by moving, he would have the opportunity to play year-round baseball."

The family moved to Seminole in 1982, and Steve immediately started playing baseball in the area. His first coach there, Clyde Collier, would remain close, and a mentor, to Steve throughout high school and college. After Collier passed away, Angela says, "Steve would hear his voice when pitching."

Steve's dad, Stratos, died five years after Steve. "I think his father felt very bad [after Steve's death]," Angela said. "He was always working and didn't get to games."

While Georgiadis wasn't able to make a huge impact while at the University of Florida, he was a favorite of his teammates—and the Gator Club Baseball Boosters, which, given his personality, was no surprise. "The boosters really loved him because he would talk to all of them," said Angela. "He didn't just show up."

Over five hundred mourners, a huge number of them from the Greater Seminole community, attended the funeral, but so did busloads of students and coaches from the college. The family received many heartfelt letters from boosters and other college officials. One noted that even though Georgiadis was sidelined after his first shoulder surgery, "he was there for every game sitting in the dugout, yelling encouragement to his teammates and taking the new pitchers under his wing." That letter described him as a "competitive player who gave his all every time he played."

Georgiadis, a Gator through and through, was buried in his game day uniform. The university retired Steve's No. 19 shortly after his death, and the boosters launched a fundraiser to erect a bronze plaque in his honor. His No. 12 was also retired at Seminole High School, where he was posthumously inducted into the Warhawks Hall of Fame; a plaque in his memory hangs at the high school baseball field. At the start of every Warhawk baseball season, a tournament is played in his honor.

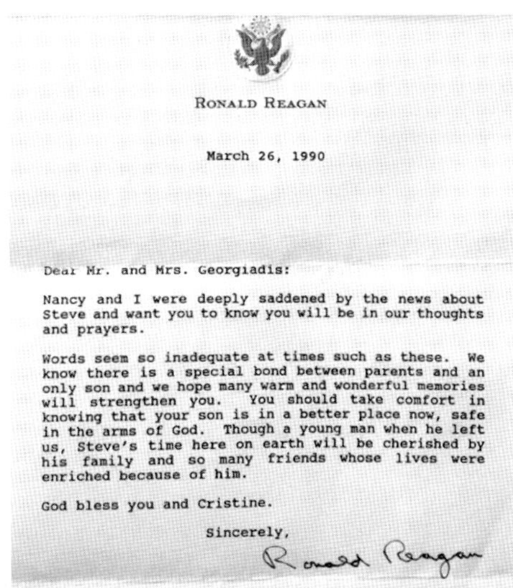

RONALD REAGAN

March 26, 1990

Dear Mr. and Mrs. Georgiadis:

Nancy and I were deeply saddened by the news about Steve and want you to know you will be in our thoughts and prayers.

Words seem so inadequate at times such as these. We know there is a special bond between parents and an only son and we hope many warm and wonderful memories will strengthen you. You should take comfort in knowing that your son is in a better place now, safe in the arms of God. Though a young man when he left us, Steve's time here on earth will be cherished by his family and so many friends whose lives were enriched because of him.

God bless you and Cristine.

Sincerely,

Ronald Reagan

Left: Among the many condolence letters received by the Giorgiadis family, the one sent by President Ronald Reagan was the most precious to Angela Giorgiadis. *Courtesy of Angela Giorgiadis.*

Below: This plaque in memory of Steve Giorgiadis can be seen at the Seminole High School baseball stadium. *Author's collection.*

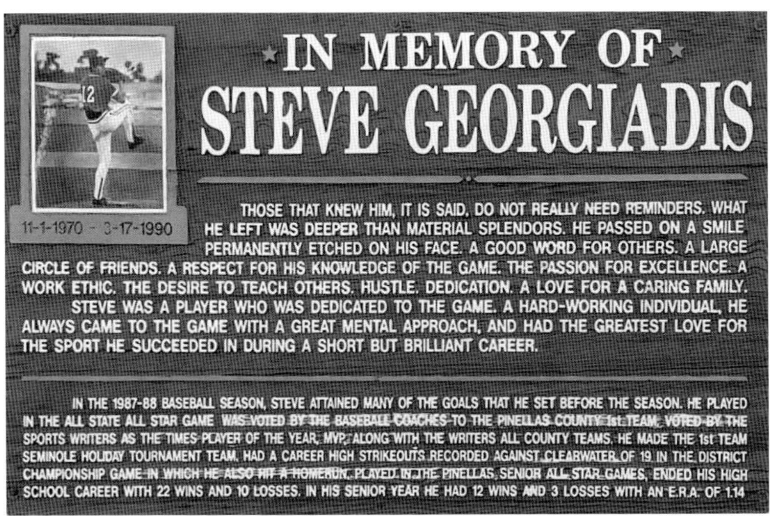

At the tournament, celebrated now for over thirty years, Angela has always been there for the opening ceremonies. Tom Kotchman is always right there with her and accompanies her onto the field. "She is a beautiful woman," said Kotchman. "Wow—I look at her and think that she is better than most, and she comes here every year. There are no words for what happened. You cannot comprehend it. It seems like it just happened yesterday. I tell the kids they have no idea what Steve did and how his life was cut short. His mother is a special person, and it's a special family. They are part of Seminole's baseball history and tradition."

When Steve died, the family received dozens of letters of condolence from friends, family, local and school officials and legislators. The one letter Angela holds particularly dear came from the president of the United States, Ronald Reagan.

There is much to remember, and much to cherish. What Angela cherishes most of all is just thinking about the ballgames and watching her son play, whether it was Little League, high school or college. "I was there for every pitch," she said.

CHAPTER 16

SURREAL YEAR

Originally published August 11, 2022

Seminole native Mike Bianco was still catching his breath a few weeks after coaching the University of Mississippi baseball team to the College World Series championship in 2022. "It's been surreal," said Bianco, a 1985 Seminole High School graduate. "It's been a busy summer. So no, it really hasn't hit me yet."

"Busy" is putting it mildly, and never more so than during a three-week span from mid-June into early July. Mississippi went from being a "bubble team" to ripping through the competition to win the NCAA national title. The Rebels finished their amazing late-season run with a two-game sweep over Oklahoma, capped by a 4–2 come-from-behind win on June 26.

On the team's return to Oxford the next day, thousands of people gathered on campus in the Grove, where the team was honored at the Walk of Champions. "It was as loud as anything I've ever heard," Bianco recalled.

There was no time to rest. Bianco took care of some business—dealing with recruiting and other team functions—and then it was on to a parade on June 29 and a celebration in the team's baseball stadium that included special guests like Mississippi Governor Tate Reeves.

After the celebration, Bianco jumped on a plane to North Carolina, where he would take on the role of head coach of the Team USA baseball squad. A few days later, he was on another flight, this one to the Netherlands for an international tournament that included teams from the Netherlands, Cuba,

Mike Bianco has been the baseball coach at the University of Mississippi since 2001. *Courtesy of University of Mississippi.*

Japan, Italy and Curaçao. "That was a great experience," said Bianco, whose team finished with a Bronze medal. "Wearing 'USA' across the chest and hearing the national anthem played was a real good feeling."

It wasn't such a good feeling earlier in the year as his Ole Miss team struggled. The Rebels started out as one of the country's top teams but then stumbled, at a low point falling to 7-14 in the Southeastern Conference. "We had nine remaining games [in the SEC], and it didn't look very good," admitted Bianco, who was an outstanding catcher in high school. "I credit the kids. The older guys held it together with their leadership. They were always confident and stayed consistent even when they struggled."

Somewhere in there was a defining moment. Suddenly they came on strong and managed to finish with a 14-16 record in the SEC. Still, getting into the NCAA tournament was far from assured. "We were probably one of the last—if not the last—teams to get in," said Bianco.

Mississippi clearly made the most of it. The Rebels won ten of eleven games in the NCAA tournament to give them an overall record of 42-23 for the year.

After twenty-plus years and many successes at Ole Miss, including several NCAA regional and SEC Western Division championships, winning the College World Series can't be beat. "This was the pinnacle," said Bianco, who had turned down offers to sign with the Red Sox and Tigers when he was younger.

The road to this "pinnacle" moment started years earlier, in Delaware. To escape the snow, his family moved to Florida, and eventually, Bianco went to Seminole High School, where he played three sports: baseball, football and basketball. He got serious about baseball starting in his junior year, making an impact as a quality player. Longtime Seminole baseball coach Bill Brinker declared that Bianco was the best catcher he had in his thirty years of coaching at the school.

After high school—and turning down an offer from the Red Sox—Bianco would continue his baseball career at Indian River Community College for two seasons; then he transferred to Louisiana State University. In his senior year, playing under legendary coach Skip Bertman, he was the starting catcher and team captain for a team that finished third in the College World Series.

After college, Bianco returned home to Seminole "to figure out my next stage in life." The next stage was short-lived, though. He took a job with an investment company in Tampa. "That lasted a couple of months, and I realized I wasn't going to be a success at that," said Bianco. "I decided that if I was going to be poor, I might as well be a poor baseball coach."

He called his old coach at LSU but was told that there wasn't anything open at the time. But Bertman referred him to Jim Wells, the coach at Northwestern State, who had an opening for an assistant.

Bertman later had a job for Bianco, and that's where Bianco worked from 1993 to 1997. In 1998, Bianco got his first head coaching job, with McNeese State, where he led the team to three straight winning seasons and an NCAA Regional appearance in 2000.

Bianco, who has over one thousand career coaching wins, took over at Old Miss in 2001, when the team was having limited success in baseball. Under Bianco's leadership, that changed dramatically—almost overnight. It took some time, but ultimately, the big payoff was winning this year's CWS.

Bianco doesn't get back "home" to Seminole as much as he'd like to these days. But he still has feelings for his old stomping grounds.

"It was a great community to grow up in," he said. "It's always been a special place to me. I lucked out growing up in that town where baseball is so important. I have a lot of fond memories."

CHAPTER 17

A CATCH AS A PITCHER

Originally published May 11, 2022

As a catcher at Seminole High School and, later, at Pasco-Hernando College, Greg Jones was a solid backstop and hitter. As a pitcher, his résumé was miniscule—in fact, less than miniscule. "I pitched maybe an inning here and there," recalled Jones. "Really, I was always catching."

Seminole's Tom Kotchman, scouting for the Angels, picked up on Jones's arm as a catcher and saw something else. "He was at a lot of our games and offered some advice," said Jones. "He just felt that I had the ability to throw a baseball. Why he thought that, I can't really say."

In his senior year at Seminole High School, Jones was drafted in the seventeenth round as a catcher, but decided he first needed "more at-bats" and went on to Pasco-Hernando. When the draft came around again, the Angels came knocking on the door once more. Jones was told he was going to be a pitcher. "All of a sudden, I adjusted my thinking," said Jones. "If the opportunity to get to the big leagues was with my arm, that was okay with me. I was excited to have the opportunity, and I did feel I had the ability to throw strikes."

Jones's professional career began in earnest in 1997 with the Angels' Single-A team in Boise, Idaho. The transition to pitcher was a lot easier for Jones than one might think. "I was comfortable right from the start," he said. "My job on the mound was to get guys out. As a catcher, I worked with pitchers, and I knew how hitters thought."

Greg Jones on the mound for the Anaheim (Los Angeles) Angels. *Courtesy of Angels Baseball.*

Making it to professional baseball was exciting, although Jones admits that while in high school, where he was a quarterback in football and also played basketball in addition to baseball, he had other ideas in mind. "I wanted to be like Deion Sanders and play football and baseball in college, then go to the pros in both sports," he said with a smile. "I thought it was the coolest thing that Deion played football in the afternoon and baseball at night! As I got older, though, I realized that Deion was different than the rest of us."

In his first season at Boise, Jones started four games but was mainly a reliever, fashioning a 2-2 win-loss record with a pair of saves. For the most part, he remained a reliever throughout his minor league career, and by the time he made it to the majors in 2003, he strictly came out of the bullpen.

Jones made his major league debut on July 30, 2003. It came in Anaheim against the New York Yankees with 43,856 fans in the ballpark. The Yankees, behind the pitching of Roger Clemens, were well ahead when Jones got the call in the top of the ninth inning.

"I will always remember my debut," said the right-hander. "I think most guys who make it to that level feel the same way. You dream about it your entire life, and you work and you work to get there. And there I was on the mound pitching against Derek Jeter, a future Hall of Famer. I got him to pop out in foul territory in right field. I will never forget that moment."

He then got Bernie Williams to ground out. After walking Jason Giambi, he caught Jorge Posada looking at strike three. "It was a cool night, all in all," Jones said.

Jones would go on to pitch in parts of four seasons with the Angels. Circumstances cut short his major league career.

"I hurt my arm in 2002," he noted. "Over time, my arm slowly got worse, and it was not the same. I tried to battle through it, but it continued to fray, and I was less effective each year. It just got tougher and tougher. Eventually, in the back of my mind, I knew it was time to retire."

On top of his arm troubles, even when he was healthy, Jones had a big challenge ahead of him, as the Angels had a powerful relief staff in the early to mid-2000s. "We had a great bullpen with a lot of depth," said Jones. "I was around a lot of dudes that got it done. The drawback for me was trying to catch on with a bullpen like that."

Jones last pitched in the majors in 2007, although he did hurl for the Dodgers Triple-A farm team in 2008. He hung up his glove following the 2008 season.

"I'm appreciative of everything that has come my way," he said. "Great parents, great upbringing. I realized a dream. Not everybody can say that."

CHAPTER 18

IN GRATITUDE TO TED WILLIAMS

Originally published March 9, 2022

Author's note: While Hector Lopez, who passed away in September 2022, six months after this interview, was technically from Pasco County, he spring trained with the New York Yankees in St. Petersburg for several years and spent a great deal of his free time in retirement visiting friends, attending games and enjoying special events in Pinellas County. He was ninety-three when he died.

Hector Lopez was close to calling it quits on a baseball career that included five pennants and two world championships with the New York Yankees—and a reputation as a player who would do whatever was necessary to help his team.

In the spring of 1969, though his major league career had been behind him for two years, Lopez was still hanging on in the Washington Senators' farm system, hoping for one last chance to make a major league roster. Then his life took an unexpected turn. New Senators manager Ted Williams approached Lopez at the team's Plant City training camp with an offer.

"How about managing our Triple-A team in Buffalo?" he asked Lopez.

"I was about to give it up," recalled Lopez, a longtime resident of Hudson who trained in St. Petersburg with the Yankees for several years. "The offer came out of nowhere. Out of the clear blue sky, and he was looking for coaches." And Lopez was in the right place at the right time.

"That's baseball for you," said Lopez.

What Lopez did not realize was that with the new job, he was making history. He would become the first Black manager at the Triple-A level. This was six years before Frank Robinson became the first Black manager in the major leagues. The fact that he was making history didn't really dawn on Lopez. "That wasn't on my mind," he said. "I just needed the work to pay the rent."

Lopez lasted only one year in Buffalo, which finished second from the bottom as a result of a shoddy roster that was handed to him. But his post–major league career continued with several scouting and coaching positions with the Yankees, capped by his final year of managing in 2008, when he helmed New York's Tampa Gulf Coast team.

Meanwhile, Lopez wasn't officially the first Panamanian to make it to the majors, but he might as well have been. He was clearly his country's first full-timer. Humberto Robinson preceded Lopez by twenty-two days. Robinson, though, had a forgettable career and played in only 102 games over a five-year major league career.

Lopez, originally signed by the Philadelphia Athletics, was promoted to the majors the same year that the A's moved to Kansas City in 1955. He had four excellent years in KC, and then his career trajectory changed dramatically in May 1959, when he was shipped to the Yankees as part of a multiplayer deal. Lopez was already having a banner season when the trade took place, and his success continued for the duration of the year. As it turned out, 1959 was Lopez's best season: he hit .283, slammed 22 homers and drove in 93 runs.

It may have been a career year with the bat, but Lopez admits he had troubles in the field: manager Casey Stengel "kept moving me around" from third base to the outfield. "I did boot a few, but that year, I made up with it with the stick," said Lopez. "Casey would move me from one spot to another. It was tough. I had to get used to it. He was a very good manager, though. He just liked to do things differently. You could get three or four hits one day, and the next day, you're out of the starting lineup. He had a lot of horses, so he could do that."

Lopez never did have another full season quite like 1959, in part because he continued to be used in various platoon roles by Stengel and, later, Ralph Houk. "I thought I would be an everyday player when I got there, but it didn't work out that way," said Lopez. "So I just did my best to try and help the team in whatever way I could."

While Lopez never matched the success of the 1959 season, he did have a career series in 1961 when the Yankees beat the Cincinnati Reds in five games in the World Series. Lopez batted .333 and drove in seven runs. He got outvoted for Series MVP by Whitey Ford, though, who won two games and set a new World Series record with $29\frac{2}{3}$ consecutive scoreless innings (that expanded to over 33 the next year). "That sure was a great series for me," said Lopez. "I really did some damage with the stick."

Lopez focuses on the good memories, although he recalls that spring training in St. Petersburg in the early 1960s had its challenges off the field for him and other Black players. "We rented a house in the colored section," he said. "We knew where to go and where not to go. We didn't go downtown and go to a movie. We stayed in our neighborhood."

Lopez finished his twelve-year career with a formidable .269 batting average, 136 homers and 591 RBIs.

"I still watch a lot of baseball," said Lopez, who at the time was still playing golf about once a week. "I'm proud to have called myself a Yankee. I root for them and Tampa Bay, of course: my home team!"

Speaking of home, Lopez was married to his wife, Claudette, whom he met at a Halloween dance in Panama in 1954, for over sixty years. The secret to that successful marriage? He joked, "A lot of 'Yes, dears!'"

CHAPTER 19

TAKE THAT, RICKEY HENDERSON

Originally published April 11, 2024

Donnie Scott was not a Hall of Famer, but he sure managed to score some "hall of fame" highlights for his scrapbook. Indeed, while he only played parts of four major league baseball seasons, Scott still chalked up a good number of pretty cool, memorable moments involving Hall of Famers—like the time he smashed a three-run homer off future Hall of Famer Tom Seaver in October 1985, or the time earlier that season when he pretty much single-handedly led the Seattle Mariners to a come-from-behind win over the Milwaukee Brewers by slugging two homers. The first one was a ninth inning tying blast from the left side of the plate off another future Hall of Famer, Rollie Fingers, and an inning later, he cracked a two-out, two-run walk-off shot against Ray Searage from the right side of the plate. His box score stats for that game were an impressive 2-for-4, two runs scored and four RBIs, including a sacrifice fly in the sixth inning.

But the one highlight that Scott remembers with an even bigger smile occurred on June 8, 1984, when he was playing with the Texas Rangers. The opponent at Arlington Stadium that night was the Oakland Athletics, whose leadoff hitter, Rickey Henderson, would eventually be inducted into the Hall of Fame after stealing a record-shattering 1,046 bases, still the all-time mark.

In that game, won by the Rangers 8–4, the catcher threw out Henderson on the base paths twice: at third base the first time, at second base the second time. "I became one of only a few guys to have thrown out Henderson twice

Donnie Scott makes a point as the manager of the Madison Mallards. *Courtesy of Madison Mallards.*

in one game," Scott proudly pointed out from his home in Pinellas Park. For the record, only nine catchers managed to throw out Henderson twice in one game during the speedster's twenty-five-year career. Scott may have been the first.

The next day, Scott was on the field getting ready for his turn at batting practice. "I'm on deck on one knee putting pine tar on my bat," he recalled. "All of a sudden, I see Rickey coming out of the third base dugout, and he's walking straight at me. I'm thinking, *What's up?* as he walks behind me and reads the name on my jersey. He's like, 'Who is this guy who threw me out twice?'"

Scott—a lifelong "Parker" who attended St. Petersburg Catholic High School for two years ("Coach Jim Vigue was the absolute best") and Tampa Catholic for two years and then was drafted by the Rangers in the second round of the 1979 draft—still laughs about the batting practice encounter with Henderson some forty years later. "It was pretty hilarious," he says.

Scott made it to the majors with Texas for a cup of coffee in 1983 and then a full season with the Rangers in 1984 before being shipped to Seattle in 1985, where he played for one season. A few years later, he saw time with the Cincinnati Reds. Scott was predominately a backup catcher.

"I didn't have the greatest success," said Scott, noting it's tough when you aren't able to play every day. "I didn't stay as long as I wanted, but I can look in the mirror and know that I played parts of four seasons in the major leagues."

After retiring from the playing field, Scott spent several years managing in the minor leagues, winning a number of league championships and a Manager of the Year award and compiling a record of 689-569. His minor league managing career ended in 2008. "I was let go by the Reds after the '08 season," said Scott. "Came back home, did some instructional work, but I wasn't sure what I was going to do."

Eventually, he heard about a managing job with a team in Battle Creek, Michigan. "I missed being around the game," said Scott. "I went there for the summer. It was a great experience on the field, but off the field—well, when I heard gunshots in the parking lot, that was enough for me."

As fate would have it, though, the Madison (Wisconsin) Mallards of the collegiate summer Northwoods League heard good things about Scott and asked him to become their manager in 2013. Scott has been with the team ever since.

"They asked me if I'd be interested, and I'm loving it still," said Scott, whose team consists of quality college players from around the country ranging from their late teens to early twenties. "Everybody is more familiar with the Cape Cod League, but I feel like our league is as good and like a rookie ball season, with a full schedule of seventy-two games. These kids learn how to deal with the grind of a long season. They all have the same goal: to get to the major leagues. I do what I can to get them ready, not just

Donnie Scott was an outstanding player in high school who later played in the major leagues. *Courtesy of Madison Mallards.*

on the physical side but the mental side, too: to make them think on the baseball field."

Of course, Scott knows that not everybody will make it to the majors, so there is more to what he offers than just baseball philosophy. "For me, this has ended up working out really well," he said. "I always wanted to be a teacher, and now I do both with these kids. What I talk to them about is not all about baseball. It's about life lessons, having a good life, having a family and kids, teaching respect for themselves and everybody else around them—the whole nine yards." On the field, he tells them, "You have to believe in yourself. Be aggressive but not cocky."

Sometimes a really special player joins the Mallards, such as Tampa native and New York Mets superstar Pete Alonso. "Someone asked me when he was playing for us, 'Do you think he'll play in the big leagues?'" remembered Scott of his then nineteen-year-old outfielder. "I said, 'He'll hit fifty damn homers.' Well, he hit fifty-three [in his rookie season]! You could see it then. He was definitely special."

Scott has not only earned two championships and a host of playoff runs with Madison, but he has also brought enthusiasm and the knack for getting the most out of all his players, not just the stars. "Donnie is an essential part of our organization," said Samantha Rubin, the team's general manager and a native of Clearwater. "Donnie is the kind of manager that players want to play for. He brings valuable experience and unmatched energy to our ball club."

"I don't have a bad day when I'm up here," said Scott, who heads to Madison mid-May for a season that starts the last week of the month. "I feel very fortunate to do this. For me, getting underneath the lights and seeing players' success—that is exciting to me. I love the organization. I love who I work for. Steve Schmitt [team owner] is the reason I'm up there. Being a manager in the minor leagues is more complicated these days. Here, they let me do what I need to do. They trust me."

Scott notes that not only are the Mallards a success on the field, they're also a big hit in the community. The team averages a league-leading seven thousand fans a game, bigger numbers than most Single-A and Double-A teams will draw on a given night.

When asked about players he found inspiring, Scott said he was always impressed with Pete Rose because of his passion for the game. Passion? Let's face it: there's no shortage of that with Donnie Scott.

CHAPTER 20

PLEASE DON'T MENTION COMPUTERS

Tom Zimmer has enjoyed a lot of great memories in his baseball career, from his playing days at Boca Ciega High School in Gulfport to catching in the St. Louis Cardinals farm system, managing a handful of minor league clubs, coaching in the Senior Professional Baseball Association and scouting for the San Francisco Giants for forty years straight.

Nothing, however, beats his stint as a catcher during the major league baseball strike in early March 1976. The owners locked out the major leaguers from March 1 to 17, so players who had already gathered in Florida for preseason drills needed to work out on their own until the strike was over. At the time, Zimmer was with the Double-A Cardinals farm team. Minor leaguers, who weren't expected to report until later in the month, were not affected by the lockout.

When the major leaguers from several teams found a home at Eckerd College in St. Petersburg to unofficially work out until the end of the lockout, Zimmer made his way down to the college and volunteered to help out. Part of the players' training routine called for game action. As luck would have it, there was a shortage of catchers. "They needed a catcher," remembers Zimmer. "They took me with open arms and let me play."

Zimmer caught live batting practice and oftentimes replaced the major league catchers in the second half of games. "That was the greatest time of my life for those two weeks," said Zimmer, whose dad, Don, had been a major league player, coach and manager. "I'm there with some of the greatest players at the time."

Members of the Pittsburgh Pirates, New York Mets, Cardinals, Cincinnati Reds, Philadelphia Phillies and other clubs participated in the

Right: Tom Zimmer with a portrait of his father, Don, in the background. *Courtesy of Tom Zimmer.*

Below: Tom Zimmer with Don Zimmer in 1987, when both were associated with the San Francisco Giants. *Courtesy of Tom Zimmer.*

workouts and games. At that time, the Mets, Phillies and Reds held their spring training camps nearby, so several of their players were in the area awaiting the end of the lockout. But other players from other teams joined in for the informal workouts. Among the numerous players on hand were Tug McGraw, Willie Stargell, Bob Forsch, Jerry Koosman, Tom Seaver and Kent Tekulve.

"It was like playing with an all-star team," said Zimmer. "All my idols. I'm warming up with them, and they're treating me like gold—just one guy after another. I'd call my dad, who at the time was coaching with the Boston Red Sox (he later became the team's manager midseason) and was waiting out the strike. I told him I'm catching Koosman and this guy and that guy. It was so cool. What a thrill. I'll never forget it."

One day, in batting practice Zimmer was behind the plate. Willie Stargell was getting ready to bat but had run out of wooden bats. Zimmer pulled out an aluminum bat used by college players and handed it to him.

"I said, 'Here, use this,'" said Zimmer. It was a heavy bat, thirty-four or thirty-five inches long. The Pirate slugger went to town.

"He hit balls with that bat like they were golf balls," Zimmer related. "The balls were just flying. He said to me, 'Look at me, I'll kill somebody with this. It's like I'm driving off a tee. No way could I use this in the pros.'"

A couple days later, Zimmer went up against Bob Forsch and smashed a home run out of the park. Zimmer remembers that hit like it was yesterday. "I'm in seventh heaven," said Zimmer. "And who's waiting for me when I cross home plate? Willie Stargell! Total heaven!"

Zimmer began his professional baseball career in 1971 after being drafted by the Cardinals in the third round. His numbers over the course of a few years weren't major league material, though, and in 1976, he became a bullpen coach with St. Louis.

"I called my dad first when they offered me the bullpen job," said Zimmer. "I didn't want to quit playing, but I figured this might be a way to stay in the game for a while."

After a year as the bullpen coach, Zimmer managed in the minor leagues, and then his baseball life took a different turn in 1981, one that didn't particularly excite him at first.

"I had just gotten let go as manager of the Salinas Angels. I called the Giants about a manager's job that was open there," said Zimmer. "I spoke to Jack Schwarz, who didn't really know me, but others [with the team] did, probably through my father. Somebody else called me back and said, 'We don't have a manager's job for you, but we're looking for a scout to cover Florida. Would you do it?' I didn't want to be a scout, but my wife was pregnant with twins, and I figured that it could lead to other opportunities."

On January 1, 1981, Zimmer officially started his employment with the San Francisco Giants. "Then it was one year to the next and forty years with the Giants as a scout, the longest consecutive run by anybody, and fifty years in professional baseball altogether," said Zimmer, with a shake of his head. "My first game was at Manatee Junior College [now part of the State College of Florida system], and my second game was at Hillsborough High School."

In those early days, many college teams started their seasons in January. Zimmer, along with several other scouts, including his longtime friend Tim Wilken, would work his way from one end of Florida to the other. "We'd do a full swing beginning in January and starting down south in Miami," said Zimmer. "We'd knock out the Miami area and work our way north."

At different times, Zimmer would catch games involving future stars like Dwight Gooden, Gary Sheffield and Alex Rodriquez.

In those first years as a scout, Zimmer noted that there were still some of the old-time scouts on the circuit, many of whom had pretty good résumés as players. "I was with the young guys," he said. "A lot of the older scouts were big league players, Yankees, Hall of Famers. A lot of them played in the 1930s and were in their eighties. But they didn't have pensions, and they worked till they died."

Zimmer was lucky. The year he joined the ranks of scouts, a pension kicked in. "Guys like Tim Wilken and me, we were in it from the bottom," said Zimmer, who retired in 2021 when he was seventy. "That saved our asses and gave us something to fall back on."

Zimmer was involved in several signings over the years but, he admits, never a first-rounder, although he did come close. Boof Bonser was ripping it up at Gibbs High School in St. Petersburg, both as a hitter and a pitcher. Zimmer had known Bonser for years and knew he had big league potential. "He played with my boys," said Zimmer, "so I saw him when he was young. He was a legend going back to when he was thirteen. He hit balls they still talk about. I did all the reports on him in 1999, and he became our first pick in 2000. That year, I went from the amateurs to doing pro scouting for the team. So I didn't get credit for the signing." But he was heavily involved years later when the Giants got all-star Evan Longoria in a trade.

When Zimmer originally started with the Giants, it wasn't the greatest scenario for a scout. "Back then, the Giants had no money," he said. "The team wasn't great, and they were playing at Candlestick. They didn't want to spend a lot of money on picks. Things got a lot better with the Giants as time went on. They did right by me."

For one year, he was on the same team as his father. In 1987, while Tom was scouting, his dad was a coach in San Francisco.

In 1989, in between major league seasons, Zimmer became a coach on the St. Petersburg Pelicans in the inaugural campaign of the Senior Professional Baseball Association. The team played at Al Lang Stadium and featured retired major leaguers over the age of thirty-five (catchers over thirty-two were eligible to play as well). "I got to see a lot of guys I saw while growing up," said Zimmer. "It was a fun league, a novelty thing. Some of the guys got shots to play in the big leagues again. I get bubble gum cards of me mailed to me all the time, people wanting me to sign them." The Pelicans won the league championship, but the league itself fell apart a short while into its second season.

Going from amateur scouting to pro scouting took a different approach and, at times, could become very intense. "I was going to the Rays games, and Marlins games, obviously, and I traveled all over, Triple A and down," said Zimmer. "We pounded those minor and major league clubs looking at who might make for a good trade. When it got near the trading deadline, you were constantly running. Those last six weeks to the trading deadline were a real bitch."

One benefit of working the pro circuit is that Tom was able to see his father more often. "I'd see him fifty or so times a year during the season," said Zimmer, noting that his father "didn't see me play baseball until I was fifteen because he was a player while I was growing up." Although, Zimmer pointed out, his dad was around to see him play football and basketball in high school.

As a catcher in high school, Zimmer took control in more ways than one since the team had a different head coach each year. "I ran all the plays as the catcher," said Zimmer, the starter behind the plate from tenth through twelfth grade. "I called every pitch. I knew more than the coaches because they were so new. I'd whisper to the coach what they should do, and they let me go with it. These days, that'll never happen. Now they wear earpieces. That's a joke to me. I have a hard time watching some of the pro games. In Little League, the coaches try and run it. Let the kids play. They need to learn some instincts. That's how my boys Beau, Ron and Lane teach their kids today."

Zimmer got his first real taste of how the games were now being handled by coaches way back in 1980 when he was managing in the

California League. One of his players was a highly touted All-American catcher. Before the player's first game, Zimmer noticed that he looked really nervous.

"I could see he was frightened!" said Zimmer. "I asked him what was wrong. He told me he had never called any pitches before, in Little League on. I said, 'Whoa, you're a pro now—you call the game.' When I was managing, I had just two signs: pitch out or bunt."

Zimmer nearly quit scouting when teams started turning to computers for updated player evaluations.

"Before then, we'd write up the reports and fax them in," recalled Zimmer. "Somebody in the office would type up the notes. In the offseason between 1999 and 2000, they told us we needed to start using computers. Most teams brought the scouts in for a one-week seminar to go over the system. Our club didn't do that. We met at the Tampa airport, and the computers came brand new, in boxes. They said, 'Do this, do that.' They told us three things: 'Plug it in and turn it on, go to the Giants website and here's the link for pro and amateur reports. Now go play with it!'"

The scouts, now tasked with operating entirely on their own, reporting everything they saw from A to Z—and still trying to master the computer program—had trouble keeping up with the daily reports. "A month into the season, nothing is coming in, and the GM is screaming, 'Where are the reports!?'" remembered Zimmer. "Every fifth day, you're supposed to be filing fifty or so reports, and I'm traveling. There was no way to keep up because you're hunting and pecking on the computer. I was up all night. I'd call my sons in college in the middle of the night and say, 'The screen is frozen! What do I do?' You were always behind. It was a terrible time. You got used to it after a while, but every two years, the security would change, and there comes a new system. It was always, always changing. I can't tell you how many times I wanted to quit."

Tom Zimmer has three World Series rings to his credit. *Courtesy of Tom Zimmer.*

The computers took a real toll on many of the older scouts. "I saw Hall of Famers get fired because they couldn't do the computers," said Zimmer. "Guys who were scouting for years. I saw it all over. I didn't like what they did to those guys."

The constant changes with computers eventually took their toll on Zimmer. "The computer is the No. 1 reason I retired," he said. "I couldn't stand it anymore. I missed going to the parks, but I don't miss the computers!"

Zimmer is still in the game, though not in the pros. "I got four grandchildren, three boys and a girl, and five nights a week, I'm the groundskeeper and help with coaching," he said.

With no reports to file on the computer, Zimmer can go home each night without a care in the world.

CHAPTER 21

SEMINOLE COACH WAS A LEGEND

Originally published October 20, 2022

The Seminole High School baseball team didn't have much of a reputation—or its own home field—in 1965 when Bill Brinker took over as the team's coach. Of course, the high school itself was only a few years old at the time, so it was still gaining its foothold in the community. But along came Brinker, and a legend was born. Brinker amassed a record of 485-217 over twenty-nine years, won conference titles, went to the state regionals several times and coached numerous players to pro careers.

"We won a lot of games, a couple of conferences," understated Brinker, ninety-six (and a half!), who now lives outside of Charlotte, North Carolina, in a senior community. "We generally had good ballclubs every year. They hustled. A lot of players I had were very good."

In his last season as coach, Brinker led the Warhawks to a 24-7 record. Clearly, his leadership set the standard for future teams to achieve. The Warhawks have won titles galore, including fifteen district championships and the 2001 undefeated national championship squad, for starters.

Rick Chapman, who was an assistant with Brinker, took over the head coaching duties in 1996. "He was an outstanding coach," said Chapman, the Warhawks' current pitching coach. "He knew how to read a kid's personality and was able to get so much more out of them because of that. He really did a great job of getting the most out of a kid's ability."

"He was a tremendous coach," said Mike Bianco, the longtime University of Mississippi baseball coach who played for Brinker. "This is a guy who was tireless. The amount of time he gave to us was just incredible, whether it was during the week, Saturdays or spring break. That El Camino was always at the field house." Brinker chuckles when the El Camino (tan, by the way) is brought up. "Yeah, it was there a lot," he says.

Bill Brinker, legendary baseball coach at Seminole High School, was camera shy and rarely had his photo taken. This photo is from a Seminole High School yearbook. *Courtesy of Seminole High School.*

His former players and coaches agree that Brinker, who also was an assistant football coach for a few years, could be tough at times. "He was strict, but you still had a lot of fun," said Tom Kotchman, who made a career of managing and coaching in the minor leagues and scouting. "That was a unique trait, and it still is."

Kotchman's first experience seeing Brinker in action was when he was fourteen years old and he went to a Seminole High championship game. "What I saw totally opened my eyes, and I was impressed how intense the game was with him as coach," said Kotchman, who played for Brinker from 1970 to 1972. "Brinker was special to me. I am very thankful to him. When I came back after college in 1977–78 and I was playing in the minors with the Reds, he let me help with the high school team. That introduced me to coaching, which I did for over forty-five years."

Chapman's first experience with Brinker was when he was a sophomore at Dixie Hollins High School. He joined a traveling summer league team, American Legion Post 104, and Brinker was the coach. "He was the first coach to give me the opportunity to pitch at that level," said Chapman.

That first outing was a rough one. Chapman had trouble getting people out. "He was yelling at me, 'You're killing me!' But after the game, he had good things to say to me," Chapman said. "That was him. He could be gruff at times. He could be in your face, but two minutes later, he's patting you on the back."

While all the wins and titles are great, perhaps Brinker's greatest legacy in Seminole baseball sprang from his determination to build a field that his team could call home. "Brink," as many called him, did some hustling himself, talking to school officials, pulling strings, reaching out to anyone who could help get this field up and going. Finally, in the early 1980s, land was allocated to the school for a field.

Once they got the land, Brinker reached out some more: to the booster club, to parents, to his players, to anyone who would get their hands dirty or could get donations of any sort. "Everything from working on the field, putting in the sprinkler system and putting up light poles, with Brinker's own hands, parents, players—that's how it got built," said Bianco, whose Ole Miss team won the national championship in 2022. "The work ethic we got from that experience was just great."

In 2016, the field was finally, belatedly, officially named after Bill Brinker. To this day, it remains arguably one of the best high school fields in the state.

After leaving Seminole, Brinker admitted, he got the itch to get back in the game. In 1997, Dave Pano, coaching St. Petersburg College's baseball team, called on Brinker to "come out of retirement."

"I love baseball, and Dave had helped me when I was at Seminole," Brinker said at the time. More recently, Brinker recalled, "I didn't have to recruit; I just worked with the players. For me, it wasn't much different than coaching high schoolers, except that the players were a little better."

These days, Brinker still has his fingers on the pulse of the game of baseball. When Bianco's team was in the hunt for the national title, Brinker kept close tabs on them and watched the games whenever he could. He roots for the Tampa Bay Rays and likes hearing about the latest news on Seminole High School and players and coaches he once worked with.

He may be living in North Carolina, but Brinker's heart is still in Seminole.

CHAPTER 22

FROM DAY ONE, SEMINOLE HIGH SCHOOL WAS NO. 1

To call the 2001 Seminole High School baseball team a powerhouse is an understatement of huge proportions. The Warhawks took the word *powerhouse* to another level.

The Warhawks were ranked No. 1 by Baseball America in its preseason poll, and that's where they remained throughout the long season. The team won thirty-one straight games, averaging nine runs a contest and winning twenty-seven of thirty-one by four runs or more. Plus a stellar pitching staff that shut down opponent after opponent, making for an amazing run.

"We were loaded," said Scott Miller, the head coach of that team. "We had a lot of good players. We started the season No. 1, and my first thought was, *How are we doing to do this all season?* We were expected to win, but we had a big target on our backs, which means everyone wanted to beat us. I never thought it was going to be a cakewalk."

They were loaded with talent, hands down. The team had several players who were later taken in the baseball draft or who attended major university programs, including Casey Kotchman, who would go on to a lengthy and very successful pro career, Bobby Wilson and T.J. Large. Other major contributors were Jon Riggleman, John Killalea, Jon Skorupski, Damon Lister, Adam Gorman and Paul Buhrow. Top to bottom, the lineup was awesome. Several players were named to various postseason all-star teams. Miller was named Coach of the Year.

The team had a major hiccup early in the season. Transfer shortstop Bryan Bass was ruled ineligible after ten games, and the Warhawks forfeited

The 2001 Seminole High School baseball team was ranked No. 1 in the country. *Courtesy of Seminole High School.*

those games. Still, Baseball America recognized Seminole as the country's No. 1 team. And that's the way most people looked at it. Later in the year, the team's leading hitter, and pitcher, Ryan Dixon needed surgery for a torn labrum and did not rejoin the team until the state tournament. As it turned out, senior Phil Stillwell flawlessly replaced Bass, Seminole overcame the loss of Dixon and the Warhawks did not miss a beat.

Wilson, the team's outstanding catcher, batted fourth in the lineup and was nearly impossible to stop at the plate. In 2001, he hit .457 with nine doubles and five homers, scored 39 runs and drove in 37. "Bobby breathed baseball," said Miller. "For sure, he was one of the best."

Kotchman, who would become one of the best defensive first basemen in major league history, hit .402 with 11 doubles and five home runs, scored 41 and knocked in 29. "We knew he was going to be a high draft pick," Miller said of Kotchman. "He was not a rah-rah guy. He was a silent leader, the quiet backbone of the team. The team could see how hard he played."

The pitching staff was led by Killalea and Large. Large went 12-0 with an ERA of 1.23. In 74 innings, he struck out 89 batters. Killalea was 11-0 with an ERA of 1.49. Killalea struck out 77 in 61 innings. Large was the winning pitcher in the state semifinal against Tate High School, and Killalea was the starter in the Class 5A final against St. Thomas Aquinas. Doing the math, Large and Killalea won 23 of the team's 31 victories.

In one of the more memorable games that season, the Warhawks came from behind to beat Dunedin, which at one point was ranked No. 5 nationally that season, 7–6 in extra innings, before an overflow crowd of an estimated one thousand people at Brinker Field.

While most of the first twenty-nine wins came pretty easily, the last two, which were played at Legends Field in Tampa (now George M. Steinbrenner Field), needed come-from-behind efforts. In the semifinal, Tate took an early 2–0 lead before Seminole exploded for six runs in the fifth inning en route to a 7–2 triumph. The Warhawks faced their toughest game of the year in the final. St. Thomas Aquinas led 4–0 into the sixth inning. Undaunted, Seminole scored four runs in their half of the sixth to tie it up. Buoyed by a balk, the Warhawks scored a run in the seventh to claim the victory and the state title, 5–4.

"In the final, we were uptight and pressing, and we came back to win it," remembered Miller. "We had our scares [at the end]. But going undefeated as the season went on was the goal."

Heading into the campaign, Miller admitted that he expected good things to happen. "I knew a lot of the dads and the Little League coaches, and I knew that they were teaching [the players] the right way," said Miller. "When I got them, they were already on their way to becoming very good baseball players."

Miller also makes the point that his assistant coach, Mike Kirkwood, played an important role in the team's success. "I always said that I was pleased to say we had two head coaches," said Miller. "Mike's a great baseball person, and he and I bounced a lot of stuff off of each other."

The ball bounced the Warhawks' way all season. Miller summed it up succinctly, calling the 2001 squad a "dream team." Who would argue with that?

The 2001 Seminole High School championship team is highlighted on a banner hanging at its home field. *Author's collection.*

Numbers Don't Lie

When you put it all together, the numbers are staggering—some might say simply amazing.

Pinellas County's Seminole High School has a long tradition of baseball success, evidenced by its fifteen district titles, eleven Pinellas County Athletic Conference championships and, of course, that undefeated memorable 2001 season when the Warhawks were crowned state and national champions.

That tradition has led to forty-four players being drafted by the major leagues, including two first rounders and seven Warhawks who eventually made it to the big time. And that doesn't include the dozens of others who may not have been drafted but went on to play for highly touted college teams, including numerous Division I programs.

Incredibly, eight players were drafted in 2001, led by first rounders Casey Kotchman (by the Angels) and Bryan Bass (the Orioles). Also selected that year were T.J. Large, Bobby Wilson (Player of the Year), Ryan Dixon, Jon Riggleman, Phillip Stillwell and John Killalea. In 2001, Bass's season was cut short due to being ruled ineligible after playing in several games.

Kotchman, arguably the greatest defensive first baseman in baseball history, and Wilson both made it to the Majors. Kotchman made his major league debut in 2004, while Wilson did so in 2008. Wilson remains active with MLB as the catching coordinator for the Texas Rangers. Five other Warhawks made

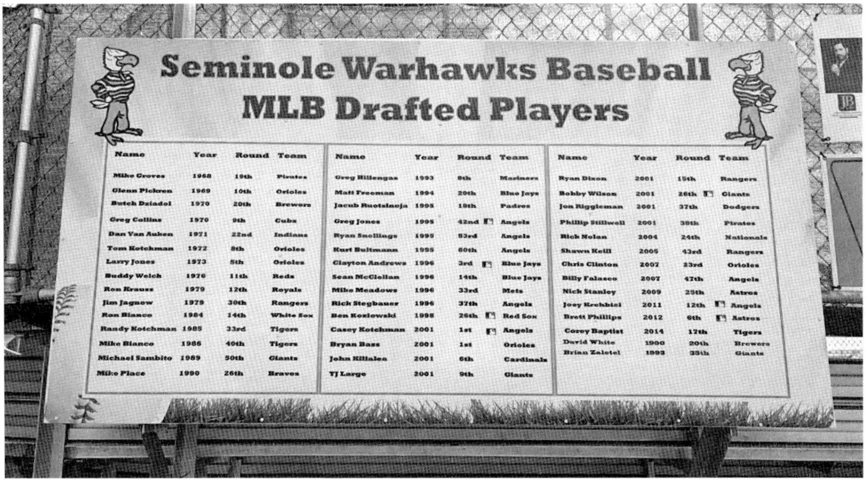

Seminole High School has had forty-four of its players drafted by major league teams. *Author's collection.*

Larry Jones was an outstanding pitcher at Seminole High School. *Courtesy of Seminole High School.*

it to major league rosters, most recently Brett Phillips, drafted in 2012 by the Houston Astros (MLB debut 2017), and Joey Krehbiel, picked by the Angels in 2011 (MLB debut 2018). Clayton Andrews, a 1996 graduate, was the first Seminole player to make it to the majors, making his debut in 2000. He was followed by Ben Kozlowski two years later and Greg Jones in 2003.

The first Warhawk to get drafted was Mike Groves, in 1968, by the Pittsburgh Pirates. Corey Baptist, selected by the Detroit Tigers, was the last, in 2014. Tom Kotchman (Casey's father), Larry Jones, Michael Sambito, David White, Rich Nolan, Chris Clinton and Nick Stanley are among the many others who were picked.

Adam Moravick, who has been the head coach at Seminole for the past several years, notes that a host of former Warhawks have not forgotten their roots and remain stalwart supporters, frequently speaking to the current players. "So many former players come back regularly and always have time to speak to the team," said Moravick, citing Tom Kotchman, Bobby Wilson, Greg Jones, Clayton Andrews, T.J. Large, Joey Krehbiel, Brett Phillips and Dontrelle Williams as a few who have talked to the team in recent times.

J.J. Baysinger, who was a senior on the 2025 team, acknowledges that when the former players visit and speak to the team, it means something. "When they come, it's like a big brother showing you that it is possible to be successful," said Baysinger, who pitched and was a catcher. "It's great, but they tell you that you still have to work hard."

The support of Seminole High School baseball goes well beyond former players. "The community support is unbelievable," said Moravick, who has been coaching in Pinellas County for over twenty years, including two as a Warhawk assistant under Greg Olsen in 2008–09. "Baseball is still very important in Seminole. Local league programs have also always been a great feeder for the baseball program, with good players and good coaches. And administrators like principal Dr. Jane Lucas, assistant principal of athletics Alana Brown and athletic coordinator Josh Walker all support the baseball program 100 percent."

Above: The Seminole High School Warhawk baseball team gets ready for the 2025 season. *Author's collection.*

Left: Seminole High School baseball coach Adam Moravick (*right*), with assistant coach (and former head coach) Rick Chapman (*center*) and booster club president Ty Dougherty (*left*). Seminole has enjoyed amazing community support over the years. *Author's collection.*

For the past few years, Moravick has been assisted on the ball field by Rick Chapman, who previously was the head coach at Seminole, as well as an assistant under legendary Warhawk coach Bill Brinker. The Seminole Baseball Booster Club is also an important part of the program, keeping players, fans and graduates up to date on current happenings on its Facebook page.

The program's successful history and highly touted coaching staff are not lost on its current players, who have their own goals. "All the coaches are really good and are really helpful," said Mack McGinnis, a 2025 senior third baseman who also played first base and pitched. "I didn't know much about the school's baseball history before I got here, although I'd heard some things about it. I know that our goals were the same as any team: win twenty games, move on to the states and win titles."

"The legacy here is great," added Baysinger. "It's just great to play here and grow as a player and to become a better person."

CHAPTER 23

EPIC MEMORIES FOR A CUBBIE

Originally published June 4, 2024

When the Arizona Diamondbacks drafted Chris Coghlan out of East Lake High School in Tarpon Springs in 2003, he had pretty much already decided that he was going to play baseball at the college level first.

As an eighteenth-round pick, 546th overall, Coghlan also realized that while it was a great feeling to be drafted, it would take a heck of a lot for him to reconsider putting off his college plans. So, he figured, let's ask for the moon. "I said I'd sign for $100,000," said Coghlan, adding that Arizona was drafting him as a catcher, which was a bit strange since "I'd never caught before."

Naturally, the Diamondbacks didn't bite at the price tag. "I was not the best player in high school," admitted Coghlan. "I didn't think anybody would want me. I didn't hit four-hundred-foot homers. I never really did anything sexy on the field."

Coghlan's thought process was also unlike others his own age. His dad died in a car accident when he was fifteen, prompting him to look at life with a different perspective. "When I grew up, I worked hard. I worked at Subway when I was sixteen," he said. "I had decided that I really wanted to go to college. Making that decision, I think, gave me an edge that benefitted me in the long run."

Coghlan went to the University of Mississippi, where he played third base and hit with precision for three years, earning SEC recognition and blossoming under coach Mike Bianco and his staff. "I am so grateful for Ole Miss and the great coaches there," he said.

Chris Coghlan, shown here fielding a ball while at the University of Mississippi, was a member of the 2016 World Series champion Chicago Cubs. *Courtesy of the University of Mississippi.*

The college route paid off when the Florida Marlins (now the Miami Marlins) selected Coghlan in the first round of the 2006 major league draft. Coghlan worked his way up from the low minors to Triple A, and on May 8, 2009, he made his pro debut. From there, it was a total dream come true that season. Coghlan, now playing second base, would hit .321 for the rest of the year with nine home runs and 47 RBIs and swipe eight bases. His .321 ranked sixth in the National League overall and first among rookies. After the All-Star break that year, Coghlan hit an astounding .372, higher than any other player during that period.

In November, he was rewarded for that effort by being named the National League Rookie of the Year. "That was never a goal of mine," said Coghlan, who now resides in Orlando. "I never dreamed of it. That's really the best individual award you could get [in baseball] outside of the MVP. I took the opportunity to share it with those people who helped me along the way: my mom, siblings, my coaches."

In the ensuing few years, injuries, starting with a knee injury, would limit Coghlan's playing time. "I tore up my knee and tried to come back too early," said Coghlan, who was traded by the Marlins to the Chicago Cubs in 2014. He started the 2014 season in the minors. "I had to fight my way back. I got a shot [in May]." He made the most of the opportunity.

In the Windy City, a much healthier Coghlan had a rebirth at the plate and put up some very productive numbers for two years, including a career-high sixteen homers in 2015. In February 2016, though, he was shipped to Oakland. It did not go well there, but then Coghlan got an early birthday present in June when he was sent back to Chicago for what would be an incredibly historical year for long-suffering Cub fans. "I had a lot of great memories playing baseball, so many great stories," said Coghlan. "But that year was, in one word, *epic*. It was the pinnacle for the Chicago Cubs, the lovable losers—108 years without a championship."

The Cubs, who had last won a world championship in 1908, defeated the Cleveland Indians in seven games after being behind three games to one. "What an amazing run that team had," said Coghlan. "We were down 3-1, yet we had that confidence in the locker room. History was made, and I was one of twenty-five dudes to be there. Just to be part of a team accomplishment like that was really something."

Coghlan's last year in the majors was 2017, when he played for the Toronto Blue Jays until mid-August, when he was designated for assignment. He did have a sensational highlight play while with Toronto (which can be viewed on YouTube). On April 25, in a game in St. Louis against the Cardinals, Coghlan broke an early 2–2 tie when he raced around the bases after Kevin Pillar hit a smash for extra bases. As he got near home plate, Coghlan leaped sideways over catcher Yadier Molina, did a somersault and scored the run. The play made every highlight reel imaginable.

Coghlan officially retired from pro ball in 2018. "That year, I got a rotator cuff injury to my right shoulder, and I wasn't the same dude," he said. "I could have tried staying around in the minor leagues hoping for another chance. But by then I knew that it was time to go and I would have to get out of fantasy world and into the real world. That wasn't easy. I prayed a lot. I had to come to grips with that. There's nothing more exciting than the sport of baseball when you go mano a mano, one on one against a pitcher. I wished it could have been more. I always had to prove my keep. It's a cutthroat business. You put up with people asking you what's wrong if you're not hitting .300. There is always someone next in line who wants your job. I had thirteen one-year contracts, so I never had a safety net. I got fired plenty of times. But I had resiliency and grit. I was faced with a lot of challenges and was hurt several times, and that limited me in achieving some of my goals. I am blessed that I played for as long as I did."

As it turns out, that resiliency and grit is what has helped make Coghlan a successful businessman. After first looking into real estate investments, he got the opportunity to help with his father-in-law's company, Orlando-based Fastening Specialists, makers of nuts, bolts, anchors, screws, washers and more. The company, which celebrated seventy years in business in 2024, continues to grow, leading to the start-up of a sister company, Big League Construction Supply, which offers all things construction-related to commercial contractors. Coghlan is the chief executive of both family-owned companies. "And we still enjoy family holiday dinners together!" he joked.

Coghlan never played for the Tampa Bay Rays, but his business philosophy is similar to theirs. "I run our businesses like a sports team," he said. "We are very culture-oriented. I look at performance metrics. You put the best talented people in the best positions, and if you do that, you grow."

Rookie of the Year, World Series ring, successful businesses: that's a Triple Crown worth talking about.

CHAPTER 24

GENERAL MANAGER: NOW THAT'S A TITLE

Originally published May 9, 2024

Author's note: In October 2024, Samantha Rubin was named executive of the year by the Northwoods League for both baseball and softball.

Growing up in Clearwater as a big sports fan and an athlete in high school and college, Samantha Rubin might have figured she would end up working for a sports team, but she might not have guessed that in a few short years, she would enter an exclusive club. In the baseball world, there have been only a handful of women in executive roles for professional baseball operations, in the major leagues and the minor leagues—or in any leagues, for that matter. Rubin counts herself as one of the few. In the spring of 2024, she was beginning her second full year as the general manager of the Madison Mallards, a member of the Midwest's elite college Northwoods League in Wisconsin.

The twenty-six-year-old, who was a righthanded softball pitcher and a power forward on the basketball court at Clearwater Central Catholic High School and, later, a member of the rowing team at the University of Florida, fell into baseball as part of an internship in her last year of college. "I was considering internships, and because it was summer, baseball was the one sport that was in season," said Rubin, who graduated from Florida in August 2019. "Someplace else [working in another sport], I would have been just sitting at a desk. I didn't want to do that. I grew up a Rays fan—and still am—so I looked at baseball and the opportunity to be a part of in-

As the general manager of a baseball and a softball team, Samantha Rubin is a recognized leader in her field. *Courtesy of Madison Mallards.*

season games and experience game day and operational functions. I also knew that in the minor leagues, I would be in a good place to get my feet wet. I did learn so much."

Rubin got her "feet wet" with the Southern Maryland Blue Crabs, first as an intern in 2019. She was hired full-time with the club in 2020 and remained with the team through the 2021 season. The year 2020, of course, was COVID-challenged, and the season was canceled. "There were only three of us on staff, and we had to pick up a lot of pieces [to keep the organization going]," said Rubin. "We did a lot of community nights on the field, drive-through proms and parades."

That year was tough, but for Rubin, it was an opportunity to put her leadership skills to use, setting the stage for more great things down the line. Ready to move on following the 2021 campaign, Rubin sent out feelers for a new job. In August 2021, she got a call from the Madison Mallards and was flown out for an interview. While she liked what she saw of the team, Rubin was hesitant to take the offer of marketing director. "I was honest with them," she recalled. "They were looking to hire a new general manager, and I just didn't want to be in the position of working under a new GM. I was also looking for a larger leadership role. So I turned down the offer."

Rubin continued looking for a new job. In the fall, she got another call from the Mallards. Obviously, they were impressed with her from the first interview, because now they upped the ante. "I got a call from [team president] Vern Stenman, and he said they still couldn't find a GM," said Rubin. "I was confused by the call. Did they want me to recommend someone? Then they offered me the job. I was like, *What?* I was shocked. I said yes!"

Actually, the agreement, which Rubin was all in on, was for Stenman to be the GM and Rubin the assistant GM that first year; Stenman would hand over the role of GM to Rubin the following year. "The idea was that I would do a season under Vern and learn everything I could about running a team," said Rubin.

In a matter of weeks, Rubin was in Wisconsin and a key member of the Mallard organization. It was December, though, and Rubin admits it was a far cry from sunny Florida. "I was flown out in August [for the first interview]. The summers are great," she said with a chuckle. "December:

that was a rude awakening. Not the easiest thing to figure out," she added during a March phone call, as snow fell outside her office window.

Mallards Manager Donnie Scott is one of many who is happy that Rubin is the team's GM. And why not? They both hail from Pinellas County! "That was pretty funny when I first met her [in August]," said Scott, the Mallards' longtime manager, who still lives in Pinellas Park. "I just about fell out of my chair when I found out she was from Clearwater."

"Donnie and I hit it off," said Rubin. "Turns out he goes to a bar, Mugs, where my dad was involved with the property."

As the GM, Rubin "does a little bit of everything" (and a lot at Warner Park's Duck Pond Stadium), from recruiting and signing players to overseeing marketing, budget, staffing, tickets, sponsorship and merch and "putting out fires every day!"

What she enjoys most about her job is the community aspect: the fans, kids, events and all that goes with that. "My strength is people," she said. "I get excited seeing kids at the game, eating an ice cream cone, having fun. I am in a cool spot here. Honestly, I'm not sure if I'd want to be a GM in the minor or major leagues. I don't want to have to deal with lawyers and contracts and negotiations. In the end, I don't really want that."

Rubin's job as the GM doubles up this year: the organization is part of the launch of a four-team women's collegiate softball league. While the baseball team plays a seventy-two-game season starting in late May, the women's team plays forty-two games starting in June. "It's exciting and new," said Rubin. "I love that I am part of this. It's the perfect timing for softball. This gives the women an opportunity to play in a minor league atmosphere."

With Caitlin Clark raising the bar in women's basketball and the start of a professional women's hockey league, there is much to be excited about. "It's incredible, such a huge moment right now for women's sports, and I want to be at the front of that," said Rubin, still athletically active herself as a CrossFit athlete. "It's a standard I want to help change. Young girls need to know that there is a path. If I can be that role model for even one person, that's a success. We've been talking a long time about changing how people view women's sports. This is the time!"

From time to time, Rubin still faces the challenges of being a GM in what is still mainly a man's world, but she shrugs them off. "At first, I'd walk into a room for a meeting, and they'd be like, 'Who is here for the Mallards?' *Me, hello.* It was frustrating, and it would bother me. Now that I've gotten more confident, I really don't think about it."

CHAPTER 25

A "RUNNING" TEAM UNDER DAVIS

When former players and associates remember Edward "Ed" Davis, the longtime baseball coach at St. Petersburg College, two things in particular stand out: his booming voice and his penchant for asking his players to run, run and run some more.

Davis retired from coaching in 1996 after amassing 692 wins and having several players drafted by major league baseball teams. Many transferred to four-year college programs, others moved on to minor league clubs and a few eventually made it to the major leagues. Among the players Davis coached who later saw major league action were Howard Johnson, Tim Teufel, Ben Hayes and Kurt Abbott. Davis was eighty-four when he passed away in January 2015, leaving a legacy that any coach would be proud of.

Jeff Davis (no relation to Ed) played for him at St. Petersburg College (at one time St. Petersburg Junior College) from 1969 to 1971. Later, he was an assistant coach with him for six years while also assuming athletic director duties starting in 1989. "Ed was like a father figure," said Jeff, who was a catcher for the Titans and, later, a baseball coach at the University of Florida. "He and his wife, Nancy, didn't have their own kids. He literally adopted his baseball players. He loved them to death."

Jeff Cesta, who has worked at the college for over thirty years and is now the director of several programs, including early education and early admissions, agreed with Jeff Davis. "He was more than just a coach," said Cesta. "He didn't have kids. The kids were his players. He kind of was like a father figure. That's what made him special."

Tim Teufel, shown here as a New York Met, was a solid hitter at St. Petersburg College. *Courtesy of New York Mets.*

"Guys really respected him," added two-time all-star Howard Johnson, who played on two world championship teams, the 1984 Detroit Tigers and the 1986 New York Mets. "He was older [than us], but he always tried to relate to us. He was a good man, honest and very communicative. You could always talk to him. I really liked playing for Coach Davis. He was tremendous."

Tim Teufel, who was also on the 1986 Mets championship team, came to St. Petersburg from Connecticut and played for Davis in 1977 and 1978. He was impressed with Davis from the start. "He was very organized," Teufel said. "He was a very driven coach and gave us the chance to perform."

"My understanding is that he was tough but fair," said Ryan Beckman, who coached at St. Pete from 2011 to 2022.

Davis did like to run, and it was a passion he shared with his players—for better or for worse! "He himself fell in love with jogging around 1970," said Jeff Davis. "At the time, it wasn't very popular. But he was very big into taking care of your body, and he'd make the players run in their Converse basketball shoes in the morning. You'd have to get up and meet him at 6:00 a.m. If you didn't jog, you didn't get to play baseball. It would be one or two miles, and you'd work up to three to four miles, and by Halloween, it was six miles. The players just hated it."

"The long-distance runs in the fall," remembered Teufel. "That was his way of weeding guys out."

"He ran with us," chimed in Johnson. "He would not ask you to do something he couldn't do. But you had to beat him, or you'd have to run again in a few days—and he did beat some guys." Johnson added, "His hair was neat, but when he ran, his sweaty hair would come loose. His long white hair would flap in the wind. We'd make fun of it. He'd sweat a lot when he ran—and in batting practice, too."

Davis had a voice right out of Hollywood. Although Beckman and Davis didn't know each other while Davis was coaching, Beckman met with the former coach on a few occasions after he took over the team. "His voice was the deepest I have ever heard," Beckman said. "The stories from his former players about the respect they had for him would say how you could hear him from miles away."

"He had a very deep voice," said Johnson. "A big, booming voice. When he was talking, it was like James Earl Jones."

In other ways, Davis, a former pitcher himself, was ahead of the curve on many fronts, including how analytics are used, now very common in the major leagues. "He was revolutionary for his time, starting fall baseball

Above: A St. Petersburg College team photo from when Ed Davis was the head coach. *Courtesy of St. Petersburg College.*

Left: Ed Davis, who retired as the St. Petersburg College baseball coach in 1996, was awarded professor emeritus status by St. Petersburg College in 2014. *Courtesy of St. Petersburg College.*

leagues through the college and with the use of analytics," said Beckman, "counting everything in the game and making decisions off that."

He'd always have his clipboard with him. Yet his game signs were simple, easy to remember. It was about playing ball and not going overboard with the numbers.

"A lot of coaches in the fall would have a two- or three-day tryout," noted Jeff Davis. "Ed's approach was different. Anybody could try out in the fall, and there would be fifty to sixty guys. He'd divide them up into three or four teams and have twenty to twenty-five intra-squad games. It was like a four-team league. By the end of October, you really had a chance to prove yourself."

While a major championship eluded Ed Davis, Jeff Davis estimated that over sixty of the former coach's players were drafted by major league baseball teams. Johnson was taken by the Tigers, Teufel by the Milwaukee Brewers and then the Chicago White Sox before signing with the Minnesota

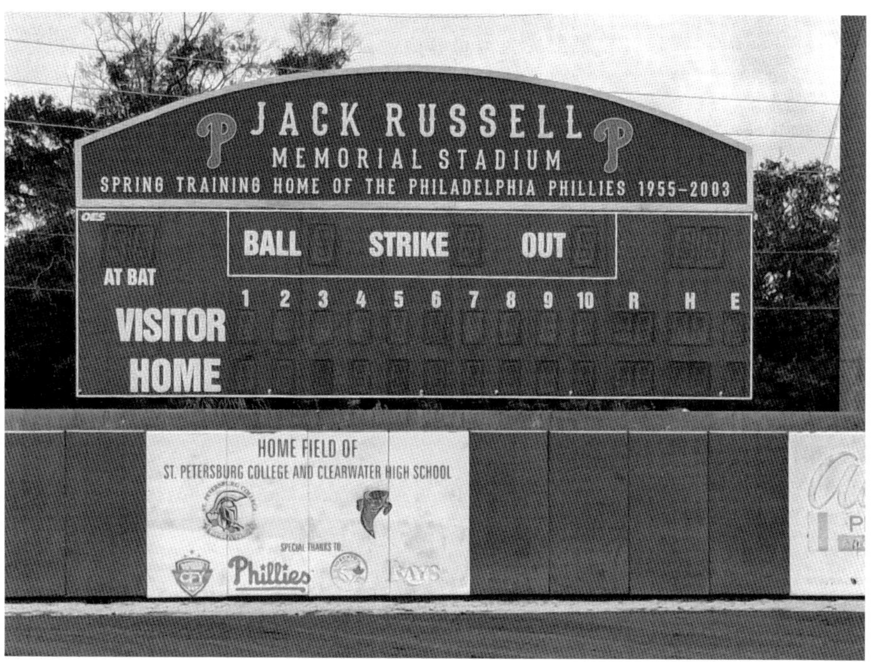

Above: Jack Russell Stadium in Clearwater was the longtime spring training home of the Philadelphia Phillies. Today it is the home park for St. Petersburg College and Clearwater High School. *Author's collection.*

Left: Jack Russell Stadium in Clearwater, the former spring training ballpark for the Philadelphia Phillies, has seen dozens of Hall of Famers take the field. Among them was Roy Halladay. *Author's collection.*

Twins. Hayes was picked by the Cincinnati Reds and Kurt Abbott by the Oakland A's. A host of others were drafted along the way, including Charles Benjamin, Bruce Irwin, Gary Bozich, Keith Feldon and Michael Clarke, who was the last Davis-coached player to be drafted—in 1995, by the Angels. In later years, Steve Lombardozzi, Bobby Wilson and Ryan Weber were three Titans who were drafted and made it to the majors.

Davis, who was also a program director for physical education at the college, was made professor emeritus by the college in 2014.

Down to his last living days, Ed Davis was still breathing baseball. "One of his sayings about baseball was you win a few, lose a few and some get rained out," said Jeff Davis, suggesting that this was also Ed Davis's viewpoint on life. "He understood the sport. If I can sum up Ed Davis, his two biggest passions were baseball—and the Florida Gators."

CHAPTER 26

UNIQUE PERSPECTIVES FROM A PR GUY

Originally published February 10, 2023

Rick Vaughn has always been passionate about his work, whether on the job with the Olympics, pro football or pro baseball. That's what led him to write the book *100 Years of Baseball on St. Petersburg's Waterfront: How the Game Shaped a City*. "I didn't intend to write a book, but I had a blast doing it," Vaughn said from his home in Palm Harbor.

The book aside, Vaughn has had a blast doing a lot of things in his sports communication career, starting with a stint working for the Washington Federals of the United States Football League and then moving on to the 1984 Los Angeles Olympics, where he was the Maryland press officer for one of the soccer sites in the United States (preliminary matches were held at various locations; the finals took place in Los Angeles). "I got to know a lot of the Baltimore media there," Vaughn said. Those relationships and his familiarity with the Baltimore area helped get Vaughn a job with the Baltimore Orioles, who he was with from 1984 to 1994. The big news during that period was the team's move from antiquated Memorial Stadium to Camden Yards. From there, it was on to the Washington Redskins as their director of communications for two years.

After Washington, Vaughn joined the Tampa Bay Devil Rays expansion team as the vice president of communications and was with them through 2016. Vaughn's time with the team, which began major league play in 1998, included the rebranding of Tampa's name, dropping "Devil" and becoming just the Rays.

A highlight of Vaughn's baseball career came when he was recognized with the Robert O. Fishel Award, named after the longtime baseball executive and given annually to an "active, non-uniformed representative of Major League Baseball whose ethics, character, dedication, service, professionalism and humanitarianism best represent the standards propounded by Mr. Fishel."

"To be linked with Bob Fishel even in a small way is meaningful beyond words," said Vaughn. "He defined the job for the rest of us, excelling while under the intense media spotlight that came from leading the PR operations of the Yankees and the American League. To have it voted on by your peers makes it that much more special."

The book project came up by chance. A couple of years ago, he parked at Al Lang Stadium during a visit to St. Petersburg. Before leaving that day, he got to wondering—and wandering. "I knew a lot about the history of baseball in St. Petersburg and the history of Al Lang Stadium, and I took a walk around the stadium to see if there were any markings," he recalled. "There wasn't much: only a bronze plaque that was put up in 1977. You couldn't even see the name of the stadium. The Rowdies"—the soccer team that plays there now—"had signage all over. I thought, 'We can do a better job than this.' So I started doing some research, which appealed to me, as I am a member of the Society for American Baseball Research."

Longtime publicist Rick Vaughn has written two books about baseball in Tampa Bay. *Courtesy of Rick Vaughn.*

Vaughn kept plugging away. "After six weeks, I fell in love with researching it," he said. "I was not planning on a book, but my wife, Sue, encouraged me, and so did my friend Tim Kurkjian of ESPN, who wrote the foreword for this book. I sent out a few proposals, and The History Press took it on."

The book includes facts, figures, stories, photos and anecdotes about Al Lang Stadium (originally called Waterfront Park) and about teams that spring trained in St. Pete, starting with the Boston Braves in 1915. The Yankees came later, as did the St. Louis Cardinals and the New York Mets. The Orioles trained there briefly as well, in the early '90s.

There were fewer than a handful of years in that heyday when St. Petersburg did not host baseball teams for spring training—by no fault of its own. Because of concerns over possible shortages during World War II, teams were discouraged from traveling far for spring training.

How did the idea of having spring training in St. Petersburg get started? It was a vision that Mayor Al Lang had way back when. He figured bringing baseball to St. Pete could make the sleepy fishing village a tourist destination.

Much of Vaughn's research consisted of perusing old issues of the *St. Petersburg Times*. "The book is intended to educate some of the newer people to the area on the history of baseball here and, at the same time, evoke memories for others," Vaughn said.

You want a taste of the kind of history Vaughn is talking about? Including two recently elected members of the Baseball Hall of Fame, Fred McGriff and Scott Rolen, 195 Hall of Famers have played at Al Lang Stadium. That list also includes the likes of Babe Ruth, Lou Gehrig, Mickey Mantle, Lou Brock, Bob Gibson, Nolan Ryan and Jackie Robinson, who attracted sellout crowds.

Vaughn would like to see the city highlight some of that history in a big way, perhaps with plaques or other markings. "We can do more," he stressed.

Author's note: Vaughn followed up his first book by writing about baseball on the other side of the Bay in Tampa Spring Training Tales: Major League Memories.

CHAPTER 27

AN IRISH BASEBALL HALL OF FAME?

Originally published April 28, 2023

There are baseball fans, and then there are baseball fans who take it to another level.

Shaun Clancy owned one of New York City's most popular sports bars, Foley's, in the heart of Manhattan, for over sixteen years. The Irish pub was filled to the brim with baseball memorabilia of all sorts and was a way station for some of baseball's biggest names, who considered it a home away from home. It wasn't unusual to see a late-night crowd including the likes of Joe Maddon, Kevin Cash, Bobby Cox, David Wright, Bryce Harper and Brian Cashman. "Anybody who was anybody would stop by," said Clancy, who bought a condo in Dunedin in 2019 and now lives in Palm Harbor.

Clancy grew up in Ireland about an hour outside of Dublin and came to the United States when he was twenty-one. He became fascinated with the Baseball Hall of Fame in Cooperstown. "I am a fan of the history of baseball and would go to Cooperstown," said Clancy, who closed Foley's during the COVID-19 crisis and permanently moved to Florida in 2020. "The more I went, I'd see names like Kelly, Duffy, McGraw—all these Irish names whose history was tied to the game."

Indeed, in the early days of professional baseball, Irish ballplayers were quite common. After one of his visits to Cooperstown, Clancy came up with the concept of the Irish American Baseball Hall of Fame. The idea was that not just big, or perhaps lesser-known, players would be elected but also people associated with the game, one way or another. The Hall of Fame was

The Irish Baseball Hall of Fame was the brainchild of Shaun Clancy. *Courtesy of Shaun Clancy.*

launched in 2008, and that first year, Connie Mack, Tug McGraw, Mark McGwire, John Flaherty and Sean Casey were inducted—as well as actor Kevin Costner, baseball writer Red Foley (yes, the pub was named after him) and New York Mets groundskeeper Pete Flynn. In 2009, among those selected were Steve Garvey, Walter O'Malley and Vin Scully.

Clancy admits he didn't take the Hall of Fame that seriously until he saw the reactions of many of the inductees. One in particular really got to him. In 2010, Tim McCarver was one of several inductees. At a ceremony in his honor that year, the former catcher and TV broadcaster (who died in February 2023) was overcome with emotion. "Tim McCarver just started crying and saying how his grandfather would be the happiest person in the world to know that he got this recognition," said Clancy. "That really changed how I looked at the Hall."

The "Irish Hall," which is now managed by the Irish American Baseball Society, selected inductees through 2019 but went on hiatus during the COVID-19 pandemic. In the summer of 2023, Clancy excitedly declared, "We are relaunching the Hall." The relaunch that year included three new inductees: Orioles hurler Jim Palmer, manager Jim Leyland and umpire John McSherry, who tragically died on the field at the start of a game in Cincinnati in 1996.

While the Hall does not have a permanent site, Clancy asserts in his Irish accent, "We haven't given up hope." Clancy added that a "long-term goal is to have an Irish team in the World Baseball Classic."

CHAPTER 28

FROM THE BIG LEAGUES TO LITTLE LEAGUE

Originally published September 27, 2024

Tim Wilken spent over forty years in professional baseball, a majority of those as a scout and major league executive looking for the next great talent to come from the ranks of high schools and colleges. Over the years, he has checked out thousands of players, but these days, he is having fun and quite content to watch one in particular, someone very close to him. "I'm chasing Little League stuff with my grandson, Jaxon," said Wilken, who retired in 2022—and, maybe best of all, in the city where he grew up, Dunedin.

Wilken, who worked for the Toronto Blue Jays, Tampa Bay Rays, Chicago Cubs and Arizona Diamondbacks in a variety of roles over the years, from scout to scouting director to national cross checker to assistant general manager, has been involved in numerous high-level signings, including Hall of Famer Roy Halladay, Jimmy Key, Vernon Wells, Gold Glover Orlando Hudson, Michael Young, Mark Hendrickson and DJ LeMahieu.

Wilken is a classic case of the local boy done good. His family moved to Dunedin from Illinois when he was twelve, and he would start at shortstop three years straight at Dunedin High School, from 1969 to 1971. "Dunedin always had a pretty good program," noted Wilken, who would later play for St. Petersburg Junior College and then Spring Hill College in Alabama.

"I was the shortstop and also pitched a little at St. Pete," he said. "I was the shortstop at Spring Hill, but one time, when our catcher got injured and there wasn't a backup, I said, 'I'll go behind the plate.'"

Tim Wilken. *Courtesy of Tim Wilken.*

In the early '70s, while going to college, Wilken worked out with the Detroit Tigers and became a batting practice pitcher. "I threw BP in the morning before classes and after school came back to pitch BP again," he said.

The expansion Toronto Blue Jays began spring training operations in Dunedin in 1977, and that year, the club had a team that participated in the Instructional League. It was actually a combined team with the Cleveland Indians, and Wilken was part of that squad. "We played about fifty-five games until around Thanksgiving," Wilken remembered. "I got fifteen dollars a day. I was rich!"

The Blue Jays' spring training games were played at Grant Field. Wilken remembers that there were trees in left field. "They had to remove the trees after the outfielders kept running into them," cracked Wilken.

Wilken also worked concessions for Toronto around that time. He later traveled some with the club and even pitched a little batting practice. One time, in 1978, he went with Toronto to Detroit. Wilken recalls it was a sweltering hot day at the old Tiger Stadium, over one hundred degrees. Jackie Moore was supposed to pitch BP. "But his arm was barking, and they asked me to pitch BP," said Wilken. "When I was done, I barely got back to the dugout. I was ready to pass out. I was borderline dehydrated. I think I drank three Cokes in ten minutes."

Wilken's life would change forever in 1979, when the Blue Jays offered him a scouting job. He would scout for Toronto for twenty-four years and then work for Tampa Bay for three, the Chicago Cubs for ten and Arizona for eight. That's forty-five years watching thousands of players, signing dozens and seeing many of them make it to the major leagues.

"I had quite a few very good signings," said Wilken. "In 1982, we signed Jimmy Key out of Clemson. He was a real good athlete and a great fielding pitcher. In 1995, it was Roy Halladay, and in 1997, we signed four guys who would have fifty-five years of major league experience between them: Vernon Wells, Michael Young, Mark Hendrickson and Orlando Hudson."

In all, Wilken noted, he was involved in the signings of thirty-four different players who would have ten years or more of service in the majors.

Of course, a few got away. "I used to say that there are fourteen closets filled with players that I missed on," he said with a laugh. "It can be humbling when you think about it."

He remembers that when he was with the Cubs in 2007, he had his sights set on left-handed pitcher Matt Moore in the eighth round. Tampa Bay, picking one selection ahead of the Cubs, took Moore. "Shame on me," said Wilken. "I should have picked him earlier. He had a lot of good years. I'm still pissed off about that one."

Wilken takes solace in knowing that other executives have missed the boat on quality players as well. "Pat Gillick, in Houston originally, told me years later that he was ready to pick Nolan Ryan, but the Mets got him," said Wilken.

Although Wilken didn't have the opportunity to draft him, the best high school player he ever saw was Bo Jackson, who first signed to play pro football and later became a two-sport pro in baseball. "I never before or since saw a guy with that kind of ability," Wilken said. "He wasn't in my scouting area, but someone told me that I had to see this kid. So I went. In a [high school] doubleheader in 1982, I saw him play shortstop in the first game, and in the second game, he pitched and had fourteen or fifteen Ks and gave up only two hits. He had a hell of an arm, could throw ninety-three, ninety-four and had a pretty good curve. And he could run. He ran the hundred-yard dash in 9.6. No one was even close."

You can certainly say that Wilken got his scouting chops from his father, Karl. Although his dad had Buerger disease, a rare condition that causes inflammation and clotting in blood vessels, he scouted part time for the Pittsburgh Pirates and the Philadelphia Phillies for over twenty-five years. Among his notable signings were Robin Roberts for the Phils and Milt May for the Pirates.

Meanwhile, Wilken's mom was as active as anybody in Dunedin and beyond. Known as the godmother of Pinellas County baseball, Claire started—and ran—the first fall league in Northern County; participating teams included Dunedin, Seminole and Clearwater. She was also involved in Babe Ruth and Little League baseball. As longtime scout and Seminole resident Tom Kotchman makes clear, "the Wilkens were a truly respected baseball family."

Wilken, along with Kotchman, was inducted into the Florida Scouts Hall of Fame in 2019. Wilken has also been recognized by many other organizations for his scouting career. When he was scouting director for the Cubs in 2012, in a true testament to his abilities and reputation, Baseball

America polled hundreds of baseball scouts around the country about who they thought was the best current scouting director in the game. Wilken was the top choice.

"If there was a scouts wing of the National Baseball Hall of Fame in Cooperstown, Tim would be in it," said Kotchman. That would be nice, of course, but Wilken, with five children and nine grandchildren, has plenty of memories with or without the Hall of Fame. "It's all pretty good," he summed up. It sure is—and has been for a long time.

CHAPTER 29

CALVARY CHRISTIAN'S SEASON OF PERFECTION

To win a championship, and certainly for a team to go undefeated, a few things have to go your way. That's the way it was for Clearwater's 2017 Calvary Christian High School baseball team.

The Warriors reeled off thirty consecutive victories en route to the Class 4A State Championship behind an awesome offense and outstanding pitching. Yet perfection is never easy, and Calvary Christian's coach, Greg Olsen, pointed out that the team's strength in many ways was its fortitude and maturity when faced with challenges. "It was a super talented team," said Olsen, who has been the Warriors' coach since being hired in 2011. "For any team to win like that, though, you have to catch some breaks. There were a number of times where we would be losing a game and something would bounce our way."

Several of the team's victories were close and could have gone another way. "If you go through our 2017 season, you see a number of one-run games that we won: 1–0, 2–1, 3–2," said Olsen. "But from the start, we were pretty focused on what we could accomplish as a team. We didn't start by saying we were going to win a state championship. As the season went along, we couldn't bury our heads in the sand. There were a few times they were pressing a little bit, but they handled the pressure great. It turned out to be a very special season."

Calvary would win six games by a run during the season, two of those in the postseason. In the district semifinal, the Warriors were deadlocked with

The 2017 Calvary Christian High School baseball team was a perfect 30-0. *Courtesy of Calvary Christian High School.*

Tampa Catholic, 0–0, until the bottom of the seventh inning, when Nolan Hudi's game-winning hit drove in the decisive run. After beating Clearwater Central Catholic 6–2 to win the district title, Calvary knocked off Trinity Prep, 4–2.

In the regional final, Calvary was down 2–0 to the First Academy into the sixth inning before rallying to win, 3–2.

In the state finals, played in Fort Myers, the Warriors left nothing on the table, defeating American Heritage in the semi, 7–1, and then, in the final, pounding Pensacola Catholic, 11–1. It was the school's first state championship in any sport.

There may have been a few close games along the way, but for the most part, the Warriors' hitting and pitching led to numerous one-sided wins. Calvary Christian averaged over seven runs a game, had nine players who played in twenty or more games batting over .300 and had a team batting average of .351. Junior Eric Kennedy led the way with an out-of-this-world batting average of .556, with fifty hits in 113 at-bats. The left-handed batting leadoff hitter smacked eighteen extra base hits (including three homers), scored forty-four runs and drove in thirty-nine. He also had twenty-six stolen bases and was thrown out only once. Kennedy could field, too. He was flawless in center field.

"That was probably one of the best high school seasons ever," said Olsen.

Catcher Matheu "Mat" Nelson, also a junior that year, hit .384; had sixteen extra base hits, including a team-leading five home runs; and drove in thirty-eight. Senior Graham Hoffman hit .372 with thirty-two RBIs and twenty-three runs scored, and senior Marco Benedettini batted .367. Justin Bench, a junior, hit .355 with twenty-one RBIs and twenty-eight runs scored.

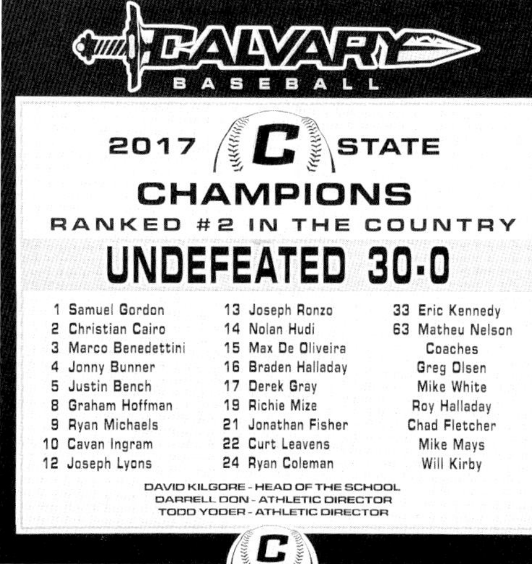

Left: The banner at Calvary Christian High School's baseball field says it all. *Author's collection.*

Below: Calvary Christian High School celebrates its 2017 championship victory minutes after the final out with a team photo. *Courtesy of Calvary Christian High School.*

Sophomore Christian Cario was also a force, with a batting average of .311 and nineteen runs scored in twenty-two games.

The pitching was just as sensational. The mound staff, led by sophomore Nolan Hudi and senior Jonathan Fisher, threw nine shutouts and held opponents to one run or less in twenty-one games. Fisher's ERA was 1.41 with fifty strikeouts, while Hudi's ERA was a miniscule 0.54 with eighty-six strike outs in 65⅓ innings. Sophomore Braden Halladay, son of Hall of Fame pitcher Roy Halladay, who died in a plane crash late in 2017, and junior Derek Gray each won four games that year.

"Our roster was really good. We had a very strong junior/senior/sophomore mix," said Olsen. "This was a team that would pretty much play together for three years in a row. So they had a lot of experience playing together. They were familiar with each other; they had friendships and strong bonds. It was a very tight group that played some great baseball, with kids that made it to the highest level of college baseball and some that were drafted by the majors. We may not have been very deep, but I'd put our starting lineup up against almost anybody."

Incredibly, Calvary Christian nearly went undefeated the next year. After going 30-0, they lost to Calvary Christian Academy in Fort Lauderdale in the final. The sixty straight wins, however, remain a high school record other teams would be hard-pressed to break. The Warriors weren't through, though. They rebounded the next year to win the 2019 state title. Some of the players from the 2017 team thus enjoyed two state championships in three years.

The Warriors Had a Special Coach in 2017

The 2017 baseball season was a very special one for Calvary Christian High School in Clearwater. The Warriors were a perfect 30-0 and captured the Class 4A state title. The team deservedly received national recognition under the guidance of Coach Greg Olsen, who took over the baseball program in 2011 after a successful run as the head coach at Seminole High School.

In 2017, Olsen had some coaching help from someone with a darn good baseball pedigree. Hall of Fame pitcher Roy Halladay, whose son Braden was a sophomore pitcher on the Warriors, was a volunteer coach that season.

Greg Olsen (*right*) celebrates the team's state championship–clinching victory with Braden Halladay (*left*) and Roy Halladay (*center*). *Courtesy of Calvary Christian High School.*

Left: Calvary Christian coach Greg Olsen celebrates his team's state championship win on the shoulders of coaches Mike White (*left*) and Roy Halladay (*right*). *Courtesy of Calvary Christian High School.*

Right: A Roy Halladay game shirt hangs at Calvary Christian High School's baseball stadium in remembrance of the Hall of Famer and assistant coach at CCHS. *Author's collection.*

Halladay, who hurled for the Toronto Blue Jays and the Philadelphia Phillies and was the author of two no-hitters (one was perfect; the other came in the postseason), tragically died in a plane crash off the coast of Pasco County a few months after the season ended.

"Roy was there a lot," said Olsen, who was also assisted by Mike White that year and for years afterward. "It was an amazing experience for our players to have him as a coach. He was so genuine and down to earth. He gave the kids feedback and advice. He loved being around the kids. He was very good to me, and I'll always cherish that opportunity to have been around him."

Halladay, an eight-time all-star and Cy Young winner in both the American and National Leagues, had a career record of 203-105 with an ERA of 3.38 and 2,117 strikeouts. Halladay, who was in the majors from 1998 to 2013, won twenty games in a season three times, and in two other seasons, he won nineteen. He was a first ballot selection for the Hall of Fame in 2019.

At the start of the 2018 Calvary Christian baseball season, a brief ceremony was held before the team's first game, and a memorial jersey plaque was presented in Halladay's honor.

A Perennial Winner Emerges

Shortly after Greg Olsen was hired as the baseball coach at Calvary Christian High School in Clearwater, he scheduled a welcome event for students who might be interested in playing on the 2012 team.

Olsen figured that taking over the program would have its challenges, and the first challenge occurred at that first meeting. "We were pretty much starting from scratch, and I knew it wouldn't be easy," said Olsen, who had come over from Seminole High School, where he led the Warhawks to several successful seasons. "It would be a fresh challenge. I scheduled the first meeting, and we had maybe seven or eight players show up."

Eventually, Olsen was able to pull together a full roster for the 2012 season. It didn't start out so well, though, as the Warriors won only two of their first nine games. But by the end, they chalked up an impressive 16-14 record. "It was like a brand new thing, and it was very rewarding to see that group of players do what they could do," said Olsen.

In Olsen, Calvary Christian got itself a quality coach with a winning résumé. At Seminole, Olsen was the coach from 2006 to 2011. During his tenure, the Warhawks captured district championships in 2007 and 2008, and Olsen's teams made the regional tournament in 2006, 2007, 2008 and 2009 and advanced to the regional final in 2010. Two future major leaguers, Brett Phillips and Joey Krehbiel, played under Olsen.

Greg Olsen, Calvary Christian baseball coach, checks out the action from the Warriors dugout. *Author's collection.*

The Olsens' decision to go to Calvary Christian was made as a family and influenced by the school's Christian values. "I was content at Seminole, and it was very tough to leave," admitted Olsen. "But my daughter was about to go to school, and I liked the vision that Calvary and its head of school, David Kilgore, offered. It was an opportunity to be part of a Christian school."

Calvary Christian was still a relatively new high school in 2011, when Olsen was hired. In 2000, it opened with thirty-eight students. Before Olsen's arrival, its sports teams had little success. The baseball team, in particular, has played a big part in the school's sports turnaround and really hit its stride in 2017, when Calvary celebrated with its sensational undefeated state championship. The Warriors finished 30-0 and captured the Class 4A State Championship. In their final high school baseball polls, Perfect Game and Baseball America ranked Calvary No. 3 nationally. MaxPreps had the Warriors at No. 5, and *USA Today* listed CCHS baseball as the ninth best team in the country.

The next two years were hugely impressive as well. The 2018 team won its first thirty games to extend its winning streak to sixty in a row, still a state record. Along the way, the Warriors earned a second consecutive district championship, a regional championship and an appearance in the 4A State Championship game—their only loss of the season. Throughout 2018, *USA Today*, MaxPreps, Baseball America and Perfect Game ranked Calvary Christian High School as the No. 1 team in the country for the majority of the spring season.

Shaking off the state final defeat from the year before, in 2019, the team continued its success, finishing 26-4 and capturing the Class 4A State Championship for its second Florida title in three years. In their final high school baseball polls, Perfect Game and Baseball America ranked Calvary No. 9 nationally. MaxPreps had the Warriors at No. 12, and *USA Today* listed CCHS baseball as the seventh best team in the country.

Olsen—who, during his tenure at Calvary, has enjoyed assistance from two former big leaguers as coaches, the late Hall of Famer Roy Halladay

Opposite: Calvary Christian baseball coach Greg Olsen. *Courtesy of Calvary Christian High School.*

Above: Calvary Christian High School's picturesque baseball field. *Author's collection.*

and Miguel Cairo—has seen several of his former Warriors players go on to major college programs, several of whom were drafted by major league baseball teams, including Johnnie Schneider, Matheu Nelson, Justin Bench, Eric Kennedy, Christian Cairo, Tommy White, Landen Maroudis and Andrew Tess. While at Seminole, Olsen also saw several of his players enjoy post–high school success.

Olsen has known personal and team success for years, starting at Countryside High School in Clearwater, where he played third base and pitched. Olsen attended Countryside from 1995 to 1998 and earned All-State recognition in 1998. Olsen was elected to the Countryside High School Athletic Hall of Fame in 1999. After high school, he attended Valdosta State University on a baseball scholarship and played for VSU from 1999 to 2002.

Olsen began his coaching career at Countryside High School in 2003 under former major leaguer Darnell Coles. In the summer of 2003, Olsen joined Terry Rupp's staff at the University of Maryland and helped coach the Terrapins in 2003 and 2004. Olsen then accepted a position at the University of Memphis in 2004, where he got to serve under longtime head coach Daron Schoenrock. Olsen coached at Memphis in 2004–05. In 2006, he became the head coach at Seminole.

Olsen wasn't sure what to expect after he took the head coaching job at Calvary Christian and that first meeting did not produce enough players for a full lineup. As it turns out, it was the start of something very big.

CHAPTER 30

DUNEDIN BECOMES A MAJOR LEAGUE CITY

Originally published April 14, 2021

Author's note: Dan Hirshberg knows his stadiums. He has seen major league baseball games in over forty stadiums in the United States, Canada and London, England. The opportunity to see a major league game in Dunedin, Florida, was something he could not pass up.

In the COVID-19 year of 2021, the Toronto Blue Jays, unable to play in Canada, took the field in Dunedin for the early part of that season before moving their home games to their Triple-A ballpark in Buffalo.

I am a baseball stadium nut. Some people enjoy coins and stamps as hobbies. Others prefer baking and gardening. Me? I go to major league baseball stadiums.

I've always had a fascination with ballparks, new and old, and every year for many years, I and three good buddies of mine (shout-out to Jerry, Dallas and Jody!) have met in a different major league city for some baseball (and music, museums and booze). As a result, I've been to places around the country I would never have ventured to otherwise, such as Detroit, Houston, Milwaukee and Kansas City.

Up until this year, sometimes with my baseball buddies, sometimes separately, I've gone to games in more than forty ballparks. In case you're thinking, *Hey, that's more ballparks than baseball cities*—note that in a few cases, I've been to multiple stadiums in the same city (for example, two Yankee Stadiums, three Atlanta Braves stadiums, etc.).

As a result of COVID-19 restrictions in Canada, for part of the 2021 major league season, the Toronto Blue Jays used their spring training stadium, TD Ballpark in Dunedin, for home games. *Author's collection.*

Which brings us to Dunedin, Florida, spring training home of the Toronto Blue Jays. Dunedin is the longtime base of spring operations for the team, as well as the location of one of its minor league affiliates. Due to Canadian COVID-19 restrictions, the Blue Jays became a team without a home for two years. The first year, they played at the home of their Triple-A team in Buffalo, where rumor had it they might be headed again in June if Canada didn't ease its travel restrictions (which is what did happen). In the first part of the 2021 season, their home stadium became TD Ballpark.

Being the baseball stadium lover that I am, I made plans to attend a game in Dunedin. I had this opportunity during the Jays' opening home series against the Angels.

Dunedin's population hovers around 36,000, far less than nearby Clearwater's 117,000 and certainly less than St. Petersburg, which is considered a small market team by major league standards. So Dunedin may not be a "major league city," but it surely is a baseball town. And while TD Ballpark is not a major league stadium, it is quaint, friendly and a joy to visit to catch a major league (or minor league) game. Everyone at the park is welcoming and obviously glad to have you join them for a night of baseball.

To be truthful, you cannot compare TD Ballpark itself to any major league park; after all, you could probably fit three TD Ballparks into the massive new Yankee Stadium. Upgraded lighting has brought its standards closer to major league levels. It's essentially a one-decker: every seat in the house is close to the action. Every pitcher's fastball can be heard hitting the catcher's mitt with a *pop*. Every crack of the bat is loud and clear, even to those sitting in the far outfield seats. When a batter gets hit with a pitch, you can almost feel it yourself. Foul balls fly over the low rooftop with regularity into who knows where on the other side. It's a mere 328 down the line, 400 to dead center.

There is no out-of-town scoreboard, no ear-piercing rock music blaring between innings, no mascot running around. It is simply a splendid place to spend a day or an evening to watch a baseball game. Thankfully, when I visited, COVID-19 restrictions were easing up, and teams were welcoming crowds back. Like many other stadiums, TD Ballpark was at a COVID-limited capacity. For Dunedin, this meant roughly 1,000 people got to come to a game (8,500 is full capacity), not including the hundreds of cutout "fans" also in attendance! Attendees were required to wear masks (when not eating or drinking) and asked to follow other safety precautions associated with the pandemic.

Dunedin itself was hoping that the Blue Jays would stick it out beyond May. One store owner pointed out that the usual crush of Canadians wasn't able to come down for spring training this year, and having the Jays here for any stretch would be another way to keep an increased flow of tourism to the area.

Seeing a major league baseball game in a cozy minor league park is pretty much a once-in-a-lifetime experience. It's worth the trip, wherever you are coming from.

My only predicament was: Do I count this as my fortieth major league baseball stadium, or am I still at thirty-nine with an asterisk?

The Author's Stadium Notes

Fast-forward four years, and the Tampa Bay Rays, as a result of extensive damage to Tropicana Field from Hurricane Helene, will be playing their

2025 season at George M. Steinbrenner Field in Tampa, the Yankees-owned stadium that is their spring training base and home to one of their farm teams in the summer. Since attending the Dunedin game, I have been to two other ballparks, upping my total to forty-two (yes, I also count Dunedin). I look forward to No. 43, Steinbrenner Field, in 2025.

In case you're wondering if any other major league teams played in a minor league stadium previously, the answer is yes. First, though, it should be noted that in 2025, the A's, formerly located in Oakland, are playing their games in a minor league stadium in Sacramento, California, in the interim before they permanently move to Las Vegas.

Besides Toronto also playing in Buffalo, the Brooklyn Dodgers played fifteen games at Roosevelt Stadium in Jersey City, New Jersey, in 1956–57. This was meant to be a threat to New York officials: the Dodgers were looking to move out of Brooklyn if they couldn't get a new stadium. New York officials didn't believe they would do it, but after the 1957 season, the Dodgers moved to Los Angeles. As an aside, Roosevelt Stadium, which was once the minor league park for the New York Giants' farm team, later hosted two Double-A minor league teams in the mid-1970s. The parent clubs were the Cleveland Indians one year and the Oakland A's the next. Among those who played in Jersey City? Future Hall of Famer Rickey Henderson.

The Giants left New York after the 1957 season as well and played two years in the former home of the Pacific Coast League's San Francisco Seals, at Seals Stadium, before heading to Candlestick Park.

The San Diego Padres spent their first few years at San Diego Stadium, former home base of the same-named Padres in the PCL.

The 1969 expansion Seattle Pilots first played in Sick's Stadium, former home of the Pacific Coast League team the Seattle Rainiers. The Pilots later became the Milwaukee Brewers.

The Montreal Expos take the cake, though. When they joined the National League as an expansion team, they played for eight years at Jarry Park, which until then was nothing more than a community field for local teams. Its capacity eventually did increase from three thousand to twenty-eight thousand.

SOURCES

Books

Clearwater Central Catholic High School Yearbook, 1979.
Gladstone, Doug. *A Bitter Cup of Coffee.* Word Association, 2010.
Golenbock, Peter. *The Forever Boys: A Second Chance to Star Again.* Carol Publishing Group, 1991.
Guinness Book of World Records. 2010.
Seminole High School Yearbooks, 1987–98 and 2000–02.
Staats, Dewayne. *Position to Win.* Advance Ink, 2015
Texas Rangers Media Guide. 2021.

Articles

Amato, Neil. "Seminole Baseball Team Won the District Title!" *The Beacon*, May 12, 1988.
Banks, Don. "Seminole's Giorgiadis Player of the Year." *St. Petersburg Times*, 1988.
Baseball Fever. "Tampa Bay Rays All-Time 40-Man Roster." October 8, 2019. https://www.baseball-fever.com.
Cairns, Mike. "Tim Wilken Is Making Pro Baseball Dreams Come True in Pinellas County." Bay News 9, February 14, 2019.
Chick, Bob. "Steve Giorgiadis Was a Craftsman, a Joy to Coach." *St. Petersburg Evening Independent*, 1990.
Chiusano, Scott. "Remembering the Most Mind-Boggling Slide You'll Ever See." MLB.com, April 25, 2022.
Cleveland, Rick. "National Champs: Ole Miss Completes Rags to Riches Story." *Mississippi Today*, June 26, 2022.

Glassey, Conor. "Times Change, but Scouting Remains the Same." Baseball America, May 30, 2012. https://www.baseballamerica.com.

Kreuz, Julia. "I Did My Share (Hector Lopez)." Sportsnet, 2019. https://www.sportsnet.ca.

NCAA. "Ole Miss Takes Down Oklahoma, 4–2, to Win the 2022 Men's College World Series." June 26, 2022. https://www.ncaa.com.

Page, Rodney. "Calvary Christian Baseball Team Opens Title Defense with Heavy Hearts." *Tampa Bay Times*, February 22, 2018.

Romano, John. "Florida Pitcher Giorgiadis Dies." *St. Petersburg Times*, March 18, 1990.

———. "Tragedy Grips Giorgiadis Family." *St. Petersburg Times*, May 4, 1990.

Schwarb, John. "Seminole Survives Perfect Season." *St. Petersburg Times*, May 21, 2001.

Thomas, Kevin. "Two Area Pitchers Toss No-Hitters." *St. Petersburg Times*, 1988.

Tompkin, Marc. "Our All-Time Rays Team." *Tampa Bay Times*, March 29, 2023.

Tribune Staff. "Georgiadis Retires 19 in Win." *Tampa Tribune*, April 30, 1988.

Van Auken, Lance. "Giorgiadis Says It All on the Mound, at Plate." *Tampa Tribune*, May 1, 1988.

Young, Pete. "Catcher Proved Most Valuable." *St. Petersburg Times*, June 20, 2001.

———. "Seminole Loses Lead but Defeats Dunedin." *St. Petersburg Times*, March 29, 2001.

News Outlets

Baseball America

The Clearwater Beacon

The Seminole Beacon

St. Petersburg Evening Independent

St. Petersburg Times

Tampa Bay Times

Tampa Bay Weekly News Group

Tampa Tribune

Websites

Baseball Reference. https://www.baseball-reference.com.

Bleacher Report. https://bleacherreport.com.

Florida Burn Tampa. https://www.floridaburntampa.org.

Irish American Baseball Hall of Fame. https://irishbaseball.org.

MaxPreps. https://www.maxpreps.com.

Miracle by the Bay. https://miraclebythebay.org.

MLB. https://www.mlb.com.

NCAA. https://www.ncaa.com.

Official Site of the Madison Mallards. https://northwoodsleague.com/madison-mallards.
Pro Housing. https://prohousing.com.
Seminole High School Warhawks Baseball/Facebook, https://www.facebook.com/seminolewarhawksbaseball.
USA Baseball. https://www.usabaseball.com.

Colleges/Schools

Calvary Christian High School
Clearwater Central Catholic High School
Clemson University
Florida Atlantic University
Seminole High School
St. Petersburg College
University of Mississippi

Special thanks to the Seminole County Public Library, Beth Lani at Clearwater Central Catholic High School, Isabel Mascarenas and Barbara Farmer-Hundt at Seminole High School, Kim Whitney at Calvary Christian High School and Jay Horwitz of the New York Mets.

ABOUT THE AUTHOR

Dan Hirshberg is an award-winning author, publicist and columnist who writes feature stories about the baseball people of Pinellas County, Florida, for the Tampa Bay Weekly News Group, highlighting pro players, scouts, managers, coaches, executives and high school and college stars. He authored a biography of Phil Rizzuto (*Phil Rizzuto: A Yankee Tradition*). For a younger audience, he's written books about John Elway, Lawrence Taylor, Emmitt Smith and Tim Hardaway. Dan is also the former sports editor of a New Jersey newspaper and has written articles for *Baseball Digest* and other publications. He has been recognized by the Florida Press Association and other industry organizations for both his writing and public relations work. Dan has the distinction of having attended major league games in every baseball city, over forty stadiums in all. To read more articles by Dan, visit https://www.tbnweekly.com.